Thank you for investing in yourself.

The only way to be inspiring is first to be inspired! Now is the time to ignite and unleash your inspiration like never before so you can maximize your ability to empower others, your relationships and your organizations.

... but <u>are you ready</u> to take life to the next level?

This book, *Think Differently*, has appeared in your life because I believe you are ready. You've been ready! You took action to get this book, whether you ordered it or you received it by attending one of my keynote leadership presentations.

Think Differently is a collection of motivational life lessons focused on helping you envision new possibility. I promise that you will feel like a rockstar and take ownership of your future like never before. I'm living proof it is possible.

I wrote this book to be a catalyst in your life and to ensure this is your best year ever. Something is about to be positively changed because you decided to take action, so be prepared to *think differently* like never before!

Receive a daily motivational quote by downloading my <u>app</u> on your phone/iPad. Simply go to your app store and find KevinCSnyder.

KevinCSnyder

Copyright © by Kevin C. Snyder, 2016

ISBN: 978-1479111725

Bulk rate discounted purchasing is available through contacting the publishing coordinator listed below or by contacting one of the
authors.

2nd Edition Edited by Write Way Publishing Company
Layout and Design by Write Way Publishing Company

www.WriteWayPublishingCompany.com
"We teach aspiring authors how to self-publish their books!

For additional information:
Dr. Kevin C. Snyder
www.KevinCSnyder.com
Kevin@KevinCSnyder.com

Follow Kevin on your social of choice

@KevinCSnyder

Interested in a special link to download my other leadership books for FREE?

Thank you for investing your valuable time to read *Think Differently*! Since we're of "like mind," I'd like to send you a special link that offers my other leadership books as free eBook downloads. Simply visit www.KevinCSnyder.com and enter your email. You'll receive an immediate response with the special link.

Also, while reading or anytime afterwards, send me a message any way you like – through email, social media, website, my app, etc. Share your thoughts, your struggles and your new-found strengths. I'd be honored to hear from you.

After you finish reading, share a testimonial! I'd love to read your thoughts which will help spread this positive message to others. Submit your testimonial on Amazon.com by following these easy steps:

#**1**: Visit www.Amazon.com

#**2**: In the Amazon search bar, type "Think Differently and Kevin Snyder" so that you find this book. Click on it!

#**3**: Then scroll down where it states "Write a Customer Review." Write your review here!

#**4**: After writing your review, send me an email at Kevin@KevinCSnyder.com and I will reply with an additional special link for FREE stuff!

Note: Although Amazon.com preferred, you can also visit my website to make book reviews/purchases or contact me directly for bulk discount orders. (www.KevinCSnyder.com Kevin@KevinCSnyder.com)

About the Author

Dr. Kevin Snyder is a professional speaker and author with a passion for helping individuals find and live theirs.

He has spoken for over 500,000 people through 1,150 presentations in all 50 states and numerous countries. His keynote audiences range from high schools & colleges to corporate organizations and associations of all types.

Before becoming a professional speaker, Kevin served as Dean of Students for High Point University in High Point, North Carolina and has worked in Student Affairs for institutions including University of South Carolina, University of Central Florida, and Embry-Riddle Aeronautical University. Kevin earned his Doctorate in Educational Leadership from the University of Central Florida and focused his dissertation research on retention factors for first-generation college students.

Kevin is also the Senior Publishing Consultant at Write Way Publishing Company, a self-publishing company he founded to help other aspiring authors become published.

Kevin is also a columnist for several magazines, a certified skydiver, scuba diver, sailing enthusiast and a former game show winner on … *'The Price Is Right!'*
Come on Down!

Dedicated to **<u>You</u>** …
you showed up which is step #1!

What happens next is up to you.

To Your Continued & Epic Success,

Kevin

*"Our future lives up to the expectations
we have for it."*

Table of Contents

Think
Differently

"You become the moment you decide to be."

Think differently – the fundamental concept within this book. Thinking different is also an essential concept for living a successful, and more importantly, a fulfilling life.

Each of us has absolute control over one thing, and that is our thoughts. The way we think determines how we feel and how we feel dictates how we act. Our thoughts manifest an outcome and our actions and behaviors can be changed at any moment simply by recognizing the power of our thoughts. No matter where you've been and where you are in life, today depends on you. Today depends on the choices you make right now.

THE PAST DOES NOT EQUAL THE FUTURE!

Today is the most important day of your life simply because you are exchanging a day of your own life for it. Why not choose to live it accordingly, with passion and purpose. Why not choose to do something different to receive a different outcome? Why not choose to think differently?

We all have a story – this book is mine. Each chapter is a different lesson about life and leadership I've learned – most the hard way. I thank God that I have been able to learn from my mistakes and become a better person as a result.

Look at the nine dots below.

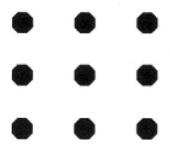

Now with your finger or a pencil, try to connect all nine dots with four straight, connected lines while keeping your finger on the paper. Each of the four straight lines must be connected to the next while not picking your hand up off the page.

Go ahead, complete this activity. Do not continue to the next page until you've spent at least one minute trying to connect all nine dots! *(Envision Jeopardy theme music here)*

Were you successful at connecting all nine dots with four straight lines?

If so, congratulations, *but* you probably have seen this exercise before during one of my presentations! If you were not able to connect all nine dots, you are not alone. I incorporate this activity in all my presentations. To date I have spoken in front of more than 1,100 groups and 500,000 people and only three people have ever successfully completed this exercise who did not know how to do it beforehand.

Below is how you would accomplish the task:

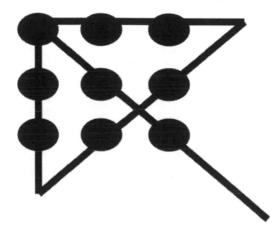

Look familiar? As you can see, in order to complete the task you must think "outside the box." Most likely you have heard this expression before, but most of us, unfortunately, do not understand how important this concept is when actually applied in life.

I believe that in order to achieve what we truly want and desire in life, we must *think differently* - outside the box. Only then will we experience life fully and accomplish the dreams to our full potential.

This area within the box is where we feel comfortable so it's natural to want to stay there. This space is an internal feeling which we associate as a "comfort zone."

We all have a comfort zone and each one is different. Some are naturally larger and some are smaller than others. However, it is when we stay within this comfort zone too long that we prevent ourselves from achieving the goals we desire and are capable of.

"The only limitations we have are the ones
we mentally place there."
~ Franklin Roosevelt, Former U.S. President

We all like to stay within our comfort zone, because, understandably it is where we feel safe. It is where we feel in control and most likely where we've been before. But again, the paradigm you must understand is that our comfort zones also place limitations on us. By not going outside our comfort zone to try new things and approaches, we are not challenging ourselves to our full potential. And more importantly, we are not achieving the goals and dreams destined for us.

"Everything you want in life is just outside your comfort zone."

Like a rubber band, comfort zones expand and shrink depending on how they are pulled. However, have you ever realized that rubber bands never retain their original shape once they've been stretched? Their shape becomes larger and larger as more tension and pull is placed on them.

Such is life. As you go outside the box to try and experience new things, as you test the boundaries of your mental and physical strength, your comfort zone expands as well - your mind is akin to a rubber band!

"More than 500 of the most successful people have said their greatest success comes just one step beyond the point at which defeat had overtaken them."
~ Napolean Hill, *Think and Grow Rich*

As you consistently take risk, try new approaches and expand your comfort zone, you slowly become more *comfortable* feeling *uncomfortable*. Most of us subconsciously avoid feeling uncomfortable at all costs – that is a natural and an intrinsic quality of our human nature to avoid discomfort and pain.

Despite this, I suggest and challenge you to change your mental association with this feeling of being uncomfortable; instead of avoiding it, consider embracing it.

At least then you will know you are testing your limits and are challenging your personal boundaries and limitations.

"You only find your limits by going beyond them."
~Roger Bannister

What would you do right now, if you knew you would not fail? Write it down:

What's keeping you from taking action towards this goal? You're clear with what it is so why not take the first step?

Is fear stopping you? Uncertainty? Fear has likely been keeping you in a comfort zone, whether you have realized it or not.

You can accomplish anything you set your mind to if you have a vision for what you decide to do. As Einstein said,

"Imagination is the preview to life's coming attractions."

If fear has been holding you back, one of the first steps you *must* take is to step outside your comfort zone. Associate feeling uncomfortable as a requirement to living your dream and achieving goals. Now that is an incredible feeling! And when you achieve and manifest that goal or intended outcome, you will want to apply this fundamental concept more and more.

It will take effort to change this neuro-association and it most likely will not happen overnight. It will take time. But like a toddler learning to walk, you will have to take baby steps to change this mental focus. Even if you fall down and feel like you can't continue, you have to force yourself to try again and again – and even then again. Remember, it's not how many times you fall, it's how many times you get back up.

Look back on how you learned to ride a bicycle. Did you successfully ride on the first attempt? More than likely, you fell down and probably even hurt yourself. Moreover, you had training wheels to prepare you for riding on your own.

Look at how you build muscle and become physically healthy. Do you build muscle simply overnight, or does it require mental and physical discipline over a period of time?

You have the power to literally alter your physical appearance by taking action and changing your diet and exercise routine. Granted, some people seem to be more genetically gifted than others in this area, but it is simply fascinating to know we can alter our bodies' physical shape and appearance when we *decide* to. This process takes time and requires dedication and sacrifice. Once it's accomplished, it's easier the next time and you feel great about the accomplishment.

I've mentioned only a few simple analogies of how anyone can change an outcome by *thinking differently* - outside the box. We have grown up hearing this cliché lesson, but why do most people not apply it in their personal lives? Most people have no understanding or appreciation for the power of expanding *comfort zones* and *thinking differently* – that is also why most of society is content with being mediocre. I do not write that statement in a negative tone. My personal definition of mediocre is status quo or an acceptance of being average.

There is nothing wrong with being average, but that is not an operational level of living I personally will accept. I do not believe my purpose in life is to be "average." I choose and aspire every day to live my life exceptionally, with passion and purpose. I know I am here to be extraordinary. So I choose to take extraordinary action. It's a choice. What will you choose?

Roger Bannister

Roger was an amazing athlete who broke the four-minute mile record in the mid-1950s. Up until that moment, it was thought humanly impossible that a human being could run one mile quicker than four minutes. Experts claimed this coveted milestone would always remain, and everyone believed it. That is, until Roger Banister.

When Roger broke the four-minute mile record, he proved it could be done. Within one year following Roger's amazing accomplishment, several other individuals broke the same record. A year after that, even more. Since then, hundreds more.

What was the difference between these two years? Was it training breakthroughs? Technology? Shoes? Supplements?

Nope. The sole reason others were able to break this record was because they *knew* it could be done. They saw that it was possible because of one person – Roger Bannister. He proved to the world that the four-minute mile was only a mindset. It was a mental limitation and boundary that he believed could be broken through. He *thought differently* and courageously leaped outside of the comfort zone which society established for everyone except him.

Wouldn't it be amazing to live daily like Roger Bannister? Imagine for one moment that every limitation and obstacle you hear about or visualize could be broken through. Envision the achievement of breaking through a barrier which everyone else sees except you. Feel the fulfillment of living your dreams before you even embark on the first step towards it.

What limitations have you placed on yourself? What are the reasons you have believed you cannot do something? What has someone told you could not be done and you believed them? What societal traditions have you accepted because no one has been able to show that it was possible yet?

Please, the next time someone tells you that you cannot do something, I want you to remember this story. Remember Roger Bannister. I want you remember that Roger did what everyone said could *not* be done. And the moment he proved it could be done, he – one person - changed history.

When you hear the phrase, "we've never done it that way" or "that won't work," please smile at that person and say "OK - thank you." Then proudly allow them to watch you do it.

There are hundreds of stories just like Roger Bannister's. In my leadership programs, you have heard me talk about many of these examples. The point is that your story is no different. You have obstacles just like everyone else. It's how you think about these challenges that will set you apart like Roger Bannister or keep you floating in the ocean of status quo.

You are reading this book for a reason. You have it in your hand for a reason. You are destined for greatness once you believe you can achieve it and are willing to embrace your power.

Jack Canfield & Mark Victor Hansen

Who are these two individuals? Most likely, you have either read or heard about their series of books.

Jack Canfield and Mark Victor Hansen are the co-editors and creators of *Chicken Soup for the Soul*, the most successful series of book lines ever published.

However, these books were not successful overnight, and in fact, the publishing of these books was nearly a miracle. What most people do *not* know is that Jack Canfield and Mark Victor Hansen went to over a hundred publishers before someone finally thought their idea might be successful. They experienced over a hundred "No's" before they finally heard a "Yes!"

The publisher who said "Yes" is the only publisher who mattered – and matters. Look now at how successful this series of books has become. It is imperative that you recognize that all it takes is one "Yes" to make all the difference in your life as well.

What would have happened if Jack Canfield or Mark Victor Hansen stopped when they were told "No?" If they did, obviously *Chicken Soup for the Soul* would not exist. Because they were determined and believed in their dream though, they knew it was just a matter of time before someone would see the potential in their idea. In fact, they expected publishers to *not* like their idea. So when the doors were shut in their faces, they were not surprised. They simply learned from it.

An invincible determination can accomplish anything.
~Jack Canfield and Mark Victor Hansen

How many attempts will you take towards your dream, towards an idea that others may or may not believe in? Will you be like Jack Canfield and Mark Victor Hansen, or will you expect the easy route and stop when you hear your first "No?"

Remind yourself that by *thinking differently*, you can have the same success as Jack Canfield and Mark Victor Hansen. These two individuals are no better than you or me; they simply persisted and believed in themselves and their dream.

How many attempts will you take to live your dream?

Michael Jordan

Michael Jordan is one of the best basketball players in history:

> NBA's Most Valuable Player: 5 times
> NBA Finals Most Valuable Player: 6 times
> Member of NBA Championship Team: 6 times
> NBA Scoring titles: 10
> All-Star: 11 times
> Slam-Dunk Champion: 2 times, 1987 and 1988
> Average points per game: 31.5 (NBA record)
> Highest points in a regular season game: 69 points
> Number of game winning shots: 25
> Games with 50 points or more scored: 37

But did you know that Michael Jordan was actually cut from his high-school basketball team? Yes, one of the world's greatest all-time basketball players was once told he wasn't good enough.

But what do you think he did when he got home that day after being cut from the team? Play video games? Complain and turn away from the sport he loved? Believe that he wasn't good enough?

Heck no.

The first thing he did when he got home was practice. He knew he was better than what the coach thought. In fact, he didn't believe the coach for one second. And for the next year, Jordan practiced constantly, shooting free throws and lay ups, getting better and better each day.

And when tryouts returned the following year, he made the team; in fact, he did amazing. He later played for the University of North Carolina at Chapel Hill; he did amazing there too. Then later played for the NBA. The rest is simply history.

The point of sharing Jordan's story is to showcase that achieving dreams and goals takes sacrifice, discipline, sweat and even tears. Nothing worthwhile ever just happens overnight. Interesting how we usually want and expect it to though.

The only reason you and I know about Jordan is because he *thought differently*. He knew he was better than what that high-school coach thought of him. He knew he would break records and be an amazing basketball star. If Jordan believed what the coach initially thought of him, he would neither have persisted nor achieved the records he did and we most likely would not even know his infamous name. What mattered to him was what *he* thought of himself, not what anyone thought of *him*.

Michael Jordan used the disbelief from others to actually empower him to become a better basketball player. I believe "he is who he is" *because* he was cut from the basketball team. He leveraged that experience to his advantage and, as a result, became an extraordinary basketball player.

Do you have the same attitude as Michael Jordan with your goals and aspirations? Do you need someone else's approval to live your dream? Has anyone ever told you that you were not good at something? Did you believe them?

The next time someone doubts you or says that you cannot do something, remember Michael Jordan's story and *think differently*. Smile at them; then proudly let them watch you do it.

Be like Mike.

To watch Michael Jordan's incredible Hall of Fame acceptance speech, simply visit http://kevincsnyder.com/free-stuff
(23 min)

Imagine you are Michael Jordan and you have the basketball. What are the chances of the ball going into the hoop if you do not shoot it?

ZERO – that's right.

When you do not take a shot, there is a 100% chance that the ball will not go in. When you take the shot, at least you have a chance. And in fact, you probably have a good chance of getting the ball in if you actually play basketball. Moreover, the more you practice, the better your chances will be. But if you do not shoot the ball, you will never know.

"I've missed more than 9000 shots in my career. I've lost almost 300 games. 26 times, I've been trusted to take the game winning shot and missed. I've failed over and over and over again in my life. And that is why I succeeded."

~ Michael Jordan

When you shoot, you at least know if the ball goes in or whether you miss. Even if you do miss you know if you shot the ball too hard, too soft, too far left or too far right. You then adapt your strategy for the next shot.

The more shots you take, the better you will be because you learn from each preceding attempt.

You always miss 100% of the shots you never take –

IN LIFE!

No one is perfect. Sometimes we take bad shots. We all make mistakes. Things don't always work out the way we hoped they would. Failure is inevitable and the irony scaring most people is that the more you try, the more failure you will likely have.

What is critical to understand and apply though is that failure and mistakes are also lessons of wisdom. When we have the right attitude, we can learn from our failures mistakes and become unstoppable for the next attempt. People who have succeeded the most recognize that failure is part of the success process! This is what we should be teaching to our youth more than anything. Take risk. Try. Learn. Try again. Fail forward. Succeed.

> *"A failure is not always a mistake.*
> *The real mistake is to stop trying."*
>
> ~ B. F. Skinner

Why are these concepts so difficult to apply in our daily lives? Why do so many of us quit so often or get frustrated when things don't go our way? We expect life to be easy but when it's not we beat ourselves up. We're much too hard on ourselves.

One of the secrets helping us apply these philosophies is that we must ask ourselves positive questions to get the results we want. Meaning, when things don't go our way, instead of saying, *"I can't believe I made such a huge mistake!"* we should ask *"What can I learn from this experience?"*

When we're stopped short of our goal or when something difficult happens to us, instead of *asking "Why does this always happen to me?"* we should replace that with *"How does this experience make me a better person?"*

This mindset is difficult at first but when you apply and live with this approach to dealing with obstacles, the world and every experience you desire is at your fingertips. You can never lose unless you give up. You can always learn something, even when you don't get your way, but only when you ask yourself the right questions.

Ask yourself a bad question, you will get a bad answer. Ask yourself a positive question, you will get a positive answer.

Happiness and fulfillment is determined by what you focus on. What you think about you bring about. We're all a work in progress, like clay, and being influential for others is as simple as understanding and applying this philosophy and approach to life. Again, you can never lose when you ask yourself the right questions. Help someone else today learn this philosophy! When they say something negative about themselves or their situation, ask them, *"What did this experience teach you?"* or *"How does what happened make you better?"* See how it works? ☺

When I worked in Student Affairs as a Dean of Students, students knew not to bring negativity into my office. When they talked bad about themselves or when they were dealing with a negative situation, I would always ask them, *"So what is the teachable moment here? How does this experience make you better?"* Then silence as I patiently waited for them to respond. Their answer would commonly lead to something much more deep, including tears and high emotions, and ultimately me asking if they would want to talk to one of our counselors down the hall. They often agreed which made me thrilled because they were dealing with the root issue and reprogramming their mind positively. To me, that's student development.

Back to you ... whether it's a bad experience at your job, a relationship ending, disappointing feedback you just received, rejection, etc. – it doesn't matter. Even when bad things happen, you still are a better person as a result because you have taken action and asked yourself the right questions.

In this chapter, we've reviewed several amazingly famous people: Roger Bannister, Jack Canfield, Mark Victor Hansen and Michael Jordan.

What do all these people have in common?

The commonality that all these examples share is that they *think differently.* Their success is a direct result of their mentality and their belief system says "never quit – keep trying." All of them consistently asked themselves positive questions even when it seemed hopeless. When others would have quit, they persisted because they learned from their failure. Their failure made them better. They also believed in their goals, took action and are remembered greatly for it.

"A great many years ago I purchased a fine dictionary. The first thing I did with it was to turn to the word 'impossible' and neatly cut it out of the book."

~ Napolean Hill, *Think and Grow Rich*

To watch a short motivational video, simply visit
http://kevincsnyder.com/free-stuff **(1 min)**

Before moving onto the next chapter, take a moment to reflect on how you feel right now. What did you learn from this chapter? What surprised you? What affirmed what you already know? List any thoughts and comments below so you can return to them at a later date:

I Lived My Dream

"You can only live a dream when you have one first."
~ Kevin Snyder

I religiously watched *The Price Is Right*, television's longest-running game show, for as long as I can remember.

Growing up, I was obsessed with the show and planned my school lunch around watching it every day. Even at college, I deliberately scheduled my classes around the show. For four years, I never had a college course at the magical hour of 11 a.m., just so I could watch Bob Barker host *The Price Is Right* every single day!

During my junior year of college, I attended a student leadership conference where I met Chris, an eccentric guy with a funny personality. We became instant friends. During one of the conference sessions, we participated in an icebreaker sharing something unique about ourselves. When it was his turn, Chris stood up and announced he had just returned from a Spring Break trip where he'd been on the *The Price Is Right* and won a gazebo!

Amazed and envious, I nearly fell off my chair! Chris had no prior knowledge of my obsession with the show. Meeting him felt like a divine sign, and I knew I was destined to be on *The Price Is Right* as well.

At that specific moment, I made the conscious decision that I too would one day shake hands with Bob Barker and be on *The Price Is Right*. I truly believed and mentally envisioned I would not only be a contestant, but also a winner. Even though I had no idea "how" to get on the show, there was no doubt in my mind that this dream would come true.

Throughout that conference, I questioned Chris about his experience and absorbed the advice he shared about being selected as a contestant. He suggested taking advantage of the time standing in line while waiting to enter the studio. "The secret," he said, "is that the producers scan for contestants before the show even starts – that is how they select 'Contestants Row'."

I learned that potential contestants who obnoxiously stand out or are in large, exuberant groups of people have a better chance of hearing those magical words, "Come on down!"

After learning all this, the "how" of my dream became clear. I was convinced that if I traveled from my home in North Carolina to California and was somehow part of a group, the producers would see the excitement in my eyes and my dream of shaking Bob Barker's hand on *The Price is Right* would manifest.

Since Chris lived in California, he agreed to be the ring leader who would organize my accomplices. We kept in touch, hoping to find an available date where I could drive across the country and enact the plan. Unfortunately, the only date we could coordinate our adventure was the same date as my own college graduation!

As difficult the decision was, I knew that pursuing my dream of being on *The Price is Right* would be incredibly fulfilling and exciting. Driving across the country and sacrificing my college graduation seemed to make my pursuit even more worthwhile.

I decided to go ... and skipped my college graduation. While my classmates were preparing to attend graduation, I was preparing to drive and meet my destiny.

Three long days and 3,000 miles after leaving North Carolina, I finally arrived in Los Angeles and met Chris and his friends. He had corralled over 20 people to go with us and help me get noticed to be selected for the show.

The next morning our car caravan headed out towards *The Price is Right* studio parking lot. I was so excited and could hardly contain myself.

As we pulled into the parking lot, I was reminded of a movie scene from *National Lampoon's Vacation* – the scene where the Griswalds travel to Wally World only to discover that the amusement park was closed!

We had a similar situation ... when we pulled into the parking lot, *The Price is Right* parking lot was *E-M-P-T-Y!*

In disbelief, I stumbled from the car and sat on the asphalt, my stomach threatening to heave up the remnants of my breakfast. A security guard appeared to inform us that Bob Barker was sick and they had cancelled the show for the remainder of the week. In front of everyone, I screamed and tears flooded down my face. My graduation ceremony had been sacrificed for nothing. My entire trip was worthless.

I had no choice but to drive back home the next day. During the drive, all sorts of crazy thoughts were going through my mind. Every emotion you can imagine came and went. At times, I would scream out loud toward the long highway road in front of me.

I'll never forget being in Tennessee, nearly home, and I heard a voice. Yes, a voice. It was more than my mind asking itself a question. I literally heard a voice out loud on Interstate 40 near Knoxville, TN and this voice was asking me a question:

"How bad do you want it?"

"How bad do I want it? Where did that come from?" I asked myself out loud. I looked around. This was a surreal moment. Nothing like this had ever happened to me before. It was a spiritual situation.

Although it scared me a bit at first, I convinced myself that it was only my mind asking itself a question – intensely. I started to think about my answer to that question. "How bad *do* I want it? How bad *do* I want it?"

The answer? I wanted it bad, more than anything else I had ever desired in my life. *The Price Is Right* was my first dream. Might seem silly to you but it was *my* dream and that's all that mattered. I had never had a dream before that seemed so clear in my mind. It was a vision that I expected to manifest and come true.

Despite my disappointment and shock from the show being canceled, my dream of being a contestant someday was only made stronger through this first failed attempt.

When I returned home, I received lots of phone calls from friends who had heard about what happened. They couldn't believe it either. I also kept in touch with Chris, knowing that I would need his help again.

I didn't understand it at the time, but I was beginning to understand and teach myself that the most important things in life require belief, dedication, and sacrifice. I still believed, I was dedicated to my dream and I was willing to take action and make the sacrifice.

Six months later, I called Chris to tell him that I was ready to try again. After picking our date and ordering tickets, I purchased a plane ticket to Los Angeles. Chris was in charge of arranging another energetic caravan of supporters to go with us.

I arrived to the airport at 11:00pm and Chris and his friends were waiting to take me straight to CBS television studios. We arrived to the parking lot at 2:00am and once again it was EMPTY! However, this time was different. It was empty because we were first in line!

Nearly eight hours later at 10:00am, with over 800 other eager contestants behind us, I noticed staff walking through the lines. This was it! My moment to convince them to select me for contestants row had arrived.

When they got to our group, one of the producers asked me, "Where are you all from?"

I inhaled and somehow babbled the 20-second version of my *Price is Right* obsession and life story. I do not remember what I said exactly. It was somewhat of a blur. I do recall the producers laughing, but they made no indication of calling my name on the show.

As they moved onto the other 800 people waiting in line, Chris rolled his eyes and said "Dude, you are crazy train for this show! I hope they do select you so you can move on with your life!" All I could do now was contain the butterflies in my stomach and wait.

A few hours later we were finally walked into the television studio. I could barely sit still as I waited for the show to begin. As *The Price is Right* theme music started, I literally closed my eyes and prayed to hear my own name called down to contestant's row.

The first contestant was called. Not me.

Contestant number two was called. Not me.

Contestant number three was called. Not me again.

With one more contestants to be called, I heard those magical words ...

"Kevin Snyder, Come On Down! You're the next contestant on *The Price Is Right*!"

To watch my "Price is Right" video where I get called down to Contestants Row, simply visit

http://kevincsnyder.com/free-stuff ***(1 min)***

Wwwhhhooooaaaaahhhhhh!! That moment was completely a blur but it's all on video which shows me wildly jumping up and down, knocking Chris to the floor. It's both hilarious and humbling to witness on video. Just visit my website to watch or type up *"Kevin Snyder meets Bob Barker"* on Youtube.com.

My date with destiny and Bob Barker had finally arrived. I was on contestants row! Because I had studied the show and knew how to play every game, I was more than confident I would soon be on stage shaking hands, and living my dream, with Bob Barker.

I did not win the first prize on contestant's row – I underbid. However on the second item, I placed a near perfect bid on a diamond bracelet ... and won! After toppling Chris over yet again in excitement, I ran onstage to Bob, shook his hand, placed my hand on my chest and relished in the surreal moment of my dream coming true.

I do not remember what happens next so, again, I'm relieved there is video that witnessing the account.

Onstage, I played "Punch-a-Bunch," a game where I could win prizes and up to $10,000 in cash. I ended up winning all the prizes which resulted in four punches on the money board. Each punch hole contained a specific amount of money. From one of my punches Bob pulled out $5,000! I won BIG ... or at least big for a kid just out of college!

My total prize winnings were the diamond bracelet, a steam vacuum, a napkin holder, a wicker basket, a milkshake maker and the $5,000! (*Note: neither the steam vacuum nor the milkshake maker ever worked!*)

After celebrating that night with Chris, I reflected on this journey of literally living my dream.

Although some may call my dream trivial, juvenile, or even crazy, my *Price Is Right* journey changed my life. It continues to impact my life each day as well. It's my signature story in my keynote presentations. Every time I share the story, it feels like the first time.

My story is not just about a game show or winning prizes. The journey I have shared with you is about taking time to identify *your* passions in life, no matter what they are or how silly they may seem. Once you identify what it is you desire and *will* accomplish, you must persistently take action to manifest it in your life. No one will do it for you.

How bad do <u>you</u> want it?

Like me, even though you may fail at times during the pursuit, it is that exact failure or setback which can teach and inspire you the most. Even when an experience is negative, frustrating and appears to be a difficult obstacle, realize that you are better for it. It is there to both *teach* and *test* you.

Whenever I'm feeling overwhelmed or pessimistic, all I need to remember are those magical words, *"Kevin Snyder, come on down!"* and I know all my dreams are attainable. All I need is persistence and faith.

I continue to live my dream now as I speak at high schools, colleges and all types of corporate groups around the country. I share my *Price is Right* story because it has a universal message that we all can relate to:

"You can only live a dream when you have one first."

What is your Price is Right?
What is your dream?

"There are 2 types of dreams; the ones we have when we're sleeping and the ones we make when we're awake."

~ Kevin Snyder

I'll close this chapter in Bob Barker fashion:

"Help control the pet population. Remember to have your pets spayed and neutered. Goodbye, everybody!"

Before moving onto the next chapter, take a moment to reflect on how you feel right now. What did you learn from this chapter? What surprised you? What affirmed what you already know? <u>List any thoughts and comments below so you can return to them at a later date</u>:

Passion

*"When you have passion for something,
you find a way to make it happen."*

~ Zig Ziglar

To watch a fascinating short clip of Steve Jobs on stage with Bill Gates talking about the importance of PASSION, simply visit http://kevincsnyder.com/free-stuff (2 min)

This chapter sheds light on my favorite concept. I believe this simple word is *the secret for living a fulfilled life*. It's the source of authentic leadership and our purpose for doing what we do.

It's called *PASSION*.

If we are not passionate about what we do, we won't be reaching our full potential nor will we be enjoying it. Passion must be the root, the foundation. If you don't love it, it'll not only show but more importantly, you won't be happy. If you're not happy doing it, then why do it?

Most of us know how to identify and set worthwhile goals. However, have you ever set a goal that eventually became less interesting over a period of a few weeks or months? Perhaps you were initially motivated but sooner than later, that motivation died just as quick as it started.

We all have been motivated before to achieve something and, indeed, we were actually interested in it. However, two weeks or two months later we are struggling to push onward and continue our efforts toward accomplishing it.

Being a motivated person is significantly different than being a passionate person. You see, motivation goes away unless we are truly passionate about the goals we envision and spend our time pursuing.

Unlike motivation, passion is a fuel that never runs empty. Pursuing a goal you are passionate about will never be cumbersome or a chore; rather it will be exciting and enjoyable to work toward. The more you pursue it, the more excited and fulfilled you become.

"All achievement must begin with an intense, burning desire and passion for something definite."

~ Napolean Hill, *Think and Grow Rich*

Goals we are passionate about are simply glorious to pursue. Yet why do we *not* invest more of our time, talent and energies toward goals we are truly passionate about? Think about it. How many hours of the day do you honestly spend doing something you love, something you are passionate about? Unfortunately, if you are like most people, you spend most of your days doing things you have to do. You will spend very little time, if any at all, on those things you are truly passionate about.

Some of you are thinking, "I am passionate about my family, Kevin."

Yes, you are and I am honored you have reflected on my question! So let's take a step back and make a caveat that loved ones, i.e. children and/or family, are one exception to my question. I know, not fair.

Although your family likely is your #1 priority, for just a moment let's focus only on you. Think about your passions outside of family. How many hours of the week do you spend on something you are truly passionate about?

Is what you spend most of your time doing what you are truly passionate about, or is it doing "something" you feel you have to do?

If you took a journal for one week, or even one day, you would easily identify what you spend most of your time doing. Moreover, I bet you would be shocked at how much of your day and week is spent being busy with things you feel you have to do. More importantly, you will identify how little time you invest on yourself and doing things you are truly passionate about and that make you come alive.

Unfortunately, most people are never challenged to ask themselves this question. Most of us are so busy with things we convince ourselves we have to do that we are just too busy to be passionate about something for ourselves.

Have you ever watched a hamster or a gerbil spinning a wheel in its cage? The hamster is moving that wheel so fast yet where is it actually going?

The hamster goes absolutely *nowhere*.

We've all felt like a hamster at times. It is natural for us to become so busy that we lose sight of what is most important in our lives. In fact, there might be days and weeks when we feel as if we do not have a choice regarding what we spend our time doing. But it's during these moments and days when we must say "no" to accepting additional tasks. It is during these times when we must <u>refuse to not have control</u> over own lives. We must say "no" to being more busy and "yes" to taking time each day, or at least each week, for ourselves. If one week just seems too crazy, then at least focus and look forward to the following week where you will have more time for you.

Do not give control of your life to something greater than you and what you believe in. Is your busy schedule truly more important than your health and well-being, your family and your success?

I challenge you to look forward to something each and every day. I tried this for a week a few years ago and it changed my life. Even though at times I have to force myself to find something, I still look forward to something every day. Try it.

What will you look forward to today? Tomorrow?

Make a list now of something you will look forward to each day for the next week. Again, this is a powerful activity and I highly recommend it. Once you identify something, anything, for each day, write what you're looking forward to and post it somewhere where you will see it. For example, place it in your car, your bathroom, on your refrigerator, your office computer. Heck, make copies and place them everywhere. Surround yourself by what will make you happy. I promise you that you will feel transformed and your days will be more enjoyable because, no matter what happens, you have something to look forward to.

Doing this changed my life several years ago. I know it will change your life because it changed mine.

You might even have to schedule this allotted time but when you do, know that it is *your time* and no one else's. Even the busiest people have 15-30 minutes each day to spend on themselves. It's just a matter of the choices we make. Every single person on our planet has the exact same amount of time each day. How they invest it is what's different.

Life is so much about our choices – what will you choose? To simply be busy all the time, or will you choose to look forward to something each day? Will you choose to be fulfilled and passionate?

Each day, you should spend 15-30 minutes on something you are interested in and passionate about.

Frequently, I have people ask me "How do I find my passion, Kevin?"

Being asked this question is one of the reasons I decided to write this book. The answer is not something I can answer for someone. I can only provide concepts that help them identify what it is for them. Our passions are so unique and each of us have our own.

However, when confronted by this question, I usually respond asking them what they enjoy spending time on. Quickly, I find that they don't know what they doing or don't feel they have time to invest on themselves. They are those "busy people" I have been referring to. They have not taken control of their life – rather, it has taken control of them.

Taking time for you each day is not selfish. You might say to yourself that you have far too many responsibilities right now or that your finances won't allow you to do anything but work. Perhaps you're in a relationship that makes it difficult or you take care of someone that literally takes up all hours of the day.

With sincere respect to your circumstances, what you've actually done is create an understandable list of reasons, why you are exactly correct. Remember, what you think about you bring about. If you are far too busy, then you are exactly right.

The question isn't, "Do you have time?" rather, it's really *"How can you make time?"*

Your reasons are really excuses you have convinced yourself about. That is, up until now.

What are the reasons *you* typically make for why you cannot do something? Many of the most common I hear are below:

I don't have time.
I don't have enough money.
I have kids and a family that need my attention.
I'm overweight.
I'm not strong enough.
I'm too old.
I'm too young.

Again, whatever the excuse, you're exactly right. When you identify reasons why you *cannot* do something, that is what your focus will surely be on. Your thoughts will perpetuate that reality.

Whether you think you can or cannot, you're exactly right.

What you focus on expands and attracts more of that same thing into your life. When you tell yourself you can or cannot do something, you will attract those exact circumstances like a magnet.

Here's another way of looking at it. Your life is consistently made up of the orders you give it. For example, what does a restaurant server bring to your table when you order a menu item and a beverage? They bring you exactly what you order! If they brought you something different, you would send it back.

This is what I am asking you to do, and possibly change, with your thinking. We all make mental orders to ourselves hundreds of times each day. We tell ourselves we can or cannot do something, thus making an "order" for our own life.

Tell yourself you don't have time and, surprise, you won't because you ordered it. Tell yourself you don't have enough money and, surprise, you don't. You ordered it. Tell yourself you are too young or too old, you are exactly right. Whatever the reason is, either positive or negative, is exactly correct because you ordered it.

So why not get rid of reasons and focus on results? Invest your mental energy on reasons why you *can* do something rather than why you *cannot*?

Unfortunately, most people spend more time and attention on identifying excuses rather than on finding creative ways to accomplish what they desire. They order excuses and that's exactly what is brought to their life.

If you are not used to applying this philosophy, it will require work at first. Eventually though, you make this mindset a habitual routine to deal with daily situations. By focusing on a positive order you will take control of your own life and will become truly a master at your focus. You will begin to see things more positively which will, in turn, attract more positive things to you. You will be a shining light in the darkness and others will be influenced by you as well. People want to follow someone who is positive and inspired. Embracing and utilizing this approach and philosophy is a personal power most will never even understand. It's time you showed them how.

"The reason most people settle for mediocrity is that they have chosen never to master something they truly love."
~ Anthony Robbins

I believe the secret key to unlocking and unleashing our potential is by understanding our passion and how we incorporate it in our life. Everyone has access to this key, in fact they hold it in their hands each day. Unfortunately, most do not know they hold it so closely, if at all. The *secret* is that it's *not a secret*.

It's your time. You can lead a more fulfilled, passionate life starting right now – *if* you decide to. Reading the rest of this book won't matter much for you unless you truly have a desire to make a change and to take control. Your *reasons* for identifying and pursuing your passion have now arrived.

I acknowledge that we all have different circumstances and some of us have more responsibilities than others which might limit how much risk we can take to make a personal, life change. Those circumstances and responsibilities do not mean we cannot make a change; rather, it just means we must consider them as we move forward.

Where some can make a 10 degree change, others can only make a 1-2 degree change. The amount of degree is irrelevant. What matters is the effort and action of simply beginning.

From now on, instead of saying to yourself, "No, I have too much responsibility," ask yourself "Yes I can. *How* can I manage my responsibilities to make time?"

When you ask yourself "*How?*", it opens your mind to creatively find the answers.

Each day, you should spend 15-30 minutes on something you are interested in and passionate about.

What can you look forward to today?

To watch an inspirational clip titled, "How bad do you want it?" by Erik Thomas- the Hip Hop Preacher, simply visit <u>http://kevincsnyder.com/free-stuff</u> **(6 min)**

Before moving onto the next chapter, take a moment to reflect on how you feel right now. What did you learn from this chapter? What surprised you? What affirmed what you already know? <u>List any thoughts and comments below so you can return to them at a later date</u>:

Lessons Of
Wisdom

*"Our greatest mistakes can be our greatest lessons
learned no other way."*

~ J.K. Rowling

---

*To watch J.K. Rowling's inspirational graduation speech where
she talks about the importance of her failures, simply visit
http://kevincsnyder.com/free-stuff* **(20 min)**

We all make mistakes – no one is perfect. In fact,
acknowledging and learning from our mistakes builds moral
character, fosters integrity and teaches incredible life lessons.

It's when we choose *not* to learn from our mistakes
when we lose the lesson that life offers to teach us.

"When you lose, don't lose the lesson."
~ The Dalai Lama

When I was a high school senior, I became president of a show choir organization called *Knightsounds*. Each year, our group traveled to Disney World in Orlando, Florida to compete in a national singing competition.

My mother was also a Math teacher at my high school and she was a chaperone on this one specific trip.

During the tournament this particular year, I became fond of a special girl in the organization. We spent most our free time together in the same group of friends.

While walking around the shops at Disney on the first day, I immediately noticed that this group was shoplifting at nearly every store we visited – and none of them ever got caught. What disappointed me even more was that the girl I liked was also the main influencer.

After the first day, I decided to simply keep my mouth shut and not say a word to anyone. I certainly did not want to get the group I was with, especially the girl I liked, in trouble. I also did not want to say anything to the group worrying they would unwelcome me from hanging around with them – and her.

At the end of the third and final day of the competition, we were given several hours of free time before needing to be back on the bus for departure. Of course, I spent this time with the girl I liked and her group of friends.

While in the final shop before heading back toward the bus, I bought a Disney t-shirt. I then waited outside for several minutes. When I returned inside the store to find out what was taking the group so long, I found them shoplifting again.

This time though, I became tempted to impress and show them I was just as clever as they were. I wanted to fit in and be cool like them. Without even thinking, I looked around, grabbed a Goofy hat and put the hat inside the same bag I had already purchased the shirt.

I looked around again to make sure no one noticed - besides the girl I liked - and then walked outside of the store. The second I put one foot outside, a hand grabbed my arm and stopped me. Next thing I saw was a police badge and a tall man who said, "Come with me."

This guy was so huge I thought he was a new Disney character. My heart skipped a beat and my legs became immediately numb.

The officer led me to the Disney security station where all my personal information was taken and I was fingerprinted. I had never felt so alone in all my life.

During my final fingerprint, my mom walked into the security room. I had already been crying but when I saw the shock and disappointment in her eyes, I started bawling.

The music director was also with my mom and they introduced themselves to the officer handling my incident.

The officer explained to them that I had been caught shoplifting.

My mom was speechless. The music director responded to the officer saying, "Kevin is the last person she would ever expect to do such a thing."

Even though the officer could visibly observe my tearful remorse and regret, he stated he was required to file the incident with authorities.

By this time the bus had already been waiting for several hours. Because of me, everyone was sitting in the bus becoming more restless and angry with each passing moment. When I finally was released in the custody of my mom, I made the longest walk-of-shame you can imagine. I walked inside that bus feeling ashamed and angry. All 53 students had been waiting for hours.

I just kept my head down in the front seat, sitting next to my mom, not saying a word.

When we stopped for gas, most everyone exited the bus to stretch. I stayed inside the bus, not wanting to talk with anyone. Just when I thought the bus was empty, someone grabbed my arm and said, "Come outside with me."

Not knowing if they wanted to punch me or just yell, I slowly walked outside expecting the worst.

I didn't know this person well – her name was Jenny. Jenny told me that everyone knew my shoplifting attempt was out-of-character and that anyone in the group I was with were the ones who should have been caught.

Even though the words she shared felt somewhat refreshing and forgiving, it did not excuse the fact that I did what I did, regardless of being caught.

Jenny invited me to sit next to her when we got back on the bus. Reluctantly I did, but I'm so glad that I did.

We talked the remainder of that 10-hour bus ride home and through the night. When our bus pulled into the high school parking lot near 7:00am the next morning, I saw the high school principal standing at the school entrance. He wasn't there to greet the bus, he was waiting for me. My dad was right behind and neither of them were smiling.

Reality was setting in. Whatever punishment I was about to receive, I knew I deserved it. The principal immediately took me to his office and asked for an explanation. I shared everything and took full responsibility. The principal suspended me for five days despite graduation being less than one month away.

I don't remember all of the details about being "grounded" at home but it was a laundry list of privileges removed - no phone, television, car, activities after school, etc.

I deserved everything. I was so ashamed and embarrassed of myself for what I had done. More importantly though, I had embarrassed my mom as a chaperone and teacher. I had also embarrassed my family's name, my entire school, my music teacher and the *Knightsounds* organization.

I learned an incredible life lesson about ethics, accountability, and the importance of considering consequences before acting. I also learned first-hand about what happens when you surround yourself by influencers that aren't positive.

Those five days I was suspended from school were tough and I hated being at home in silence. My parents knew I was beating myself up pretty bad so called me several times each day to check up on me. After school each day friends would also stop by to check up on me. I learned who my *real* friends were.

No one from the shoplifting group, including the girl I *had* liked, ever stopped by. Not that they had any responsibility for my actions but for the first time in my life, I learned a lesson about authentic friendship. You should never lead or follow friends down the wrong path.

Jenny visited me every day, too. We formed a relationship that, even until today, was one of the most powerful relationships I have ever had. Jenny would eventually become my high school sweetheart. She saw me at my worst and was willing to look beyond it. She accepted me because she knew I was better than my mistake.

When I returned to school after my five days of suspension, it felt just plain weird. I felt like an alien from planet *Zorkon*. Of course everyone knew what I had done, including teachers and other students. The school newspaper had run a front page article about what I had done.

On the first day back, I asked the music director if I could share a few words with the group during our meeting. I had written some remarks expressing my sincere apologies and remorse for my selfish behavior. I also volunteered to remove myself as president of the group.

I still have this written speech in my diary. It was a life-changing moment and the first time I remember ever taking responsibility in a group setting.

After making my speech, no one said a word. I didn't make the speech wanting anyone to respond. I just sat down and stared at paint on the wall hoping the music director would quickly start practice. The awkward silence in the room remained though. No one, including the music director, knew what to do or say.

Finally, a voice in the back of the room spoke up and, even now, more than 20 years later, I still remember every word she shared:

> *"Kevin, speaking to us took courage. Unlike others in this same room, you took responsibility for your actions. Yes, you made a bad decision and got caught. However, you have taught us all to own a mistake. That's a powerful lesson that shows what leadership is about. I don't want you to step down as President."*

The room erupted in applause. I was shocked. I didn't know whether to smile or cry. So I did both consumed by the power of the moment.

Although not the focus of this chapter, I feel compelled to share that neither the girl I *had* liked - before Jenny of course - nor the group of shoplifters I was with during that Disney trip ever talked to me again. They ignored me. It's as if they felt the same embarrassment as I did but they didn't have the opportunity to acknowledge it in front of others. Or they didn't care to.

Hopefully they learned the same lesson as I did though.

Our teachable moments can, and should, serve as lessons of wisdom for others as well.

Even though my school problems seemed to be over, the legal problems were just beginning. Disney did press charges and I had to obtain legal representation. I pleaded guilty. It was pretty straight forward what I had done.

My lawyer was able to reduce the court charge to a misdemeanor based on my prior clean record. Since I was only 17, my record would not show the arrest. It would be expunged once I turned 18 as long as nothing else was added. Thankfully, the legal consequences of this experience would not be a permanent scarlet letter on my life.

The attorney cost was $2,000. Even though I had a great neighborhood lawn business and could pay this amount upfront, I wanted to make that $2,000 back somehow so that I would never notice it missing from my bank account. I felt that earning an additional $2,000 through a second job would help me put the experience behind me more quickly.

I began working as a waiter at Pizza Inn restaurant that summer just down the street. I kept a log during each work shift, documenting every hour worked and each tip made. Every dollar bill was saved on my bedroom desk, piling higher and higher each week. My log showed that I averaged $14.28 per hour, earning over $2,000 within two months.

I was surprised to make that much money so quickly, and frankly, so easily. Not everyone at that restaurant did as well as I did - and I was only temporary. I enjoyed the job though and meeting so many new people each shift was fun.

Once I finally earned $2,000, I told my dad. I asked him to take me to the bank with the cash piles of $1's, $5's, $10's and $20's. I'll never forget the bank teller looking at me quite awkwardly when I handed over $1100 to her just in $1's!

After I deposited the money, my dad and I went out for lunch. We talked about how good it felt that my shoplifting experience had finally reached a stage of closure – I felt able to move on. I remember him asking me, "So what did you learn from this experience?"

As I answered him, it struck me how much I had learned. Lessons of accountability, consequences, reputation, influence, relationships, leadership and much more.

Also, I talked to him how much I enjoyed being a waiter. When he asked when I was going to quit, I replied to him that I wasn't – I actually enjoyed being a waiter so much that I was going to continue working at the restaurant. I enjoyed working with people too much and helping ensure customers had a great experience at the restaurant.

For the first time in my life, I realized how important it was for me to work with, and be surrounded by, *people*. Prior to this experience, the only job I ever had was my lawn business, which was a solitary and monotonous job of walking around in circles. The money was incredible but there was no true fulfillment or interaction with anyone.

In addition to the lawn business, I found a new serving job at an upscale restaurant across town. I did very well there as well, but most importantly, I looked forward to working each day. It was clearly apparent to me that my personality was designed to work with, and be surrounded by, people – that is <u>Lesson #2</u> learned from my shoplifting experience.

<u>Lesson #1</u> was about accountability and responsibility. When you make mistakes, own it. Not only must you acknowledge a mistake, but you must also learn from it. Everyone makes mistakes, but to repeat them is no excuse. Allow mistakes to serve as lessons of wisdom so that you can be a *better* person, not a *bitter* person.

Mistakes are a part of being human. Appreciate your mistakes for what they are: precious life lessons that sometimes can only be learned the hard way.

I learned the hard way about accountability and responsibility – but the important fact is that I learned. I also learned at a time in my life when the consequences would not be as devastating as they would be now. For that I am grateful.

<u>Lesson #3</u> was a hidden gem – Jenny. We dated for nearly two years. I would not have met her if it were not for the shoplifting experience. Not only did she appear in my life during an incredibly difficult time, but she was there for me when others were not. She accepted my faults and bad judgments, but more importantly, she helped me realize my decision was not reflective of who I was. Rather, it was simply a poor decision I learned from.

Looking back on this entire experience, I am amazed and grateful to have learned so much. I am a better person as a result of it, but only because I allowed this to be a lesson of wisdom.

Never regret anything that has happened in your life. It's led you to where you are today. It cannot be changed, undone or forgotten. Take it as a lesson learned and move on. Your scars are beautiful. Bloom where you are planted.

*To watch a very special inspirational video titled, "The Truth!", visit http://kevincsnyder.com/free-stuff **(2 min)***

Before moving onto the next chapter, take a moment to reflect on how you feel right now. What did you learn from this chapter? What surprised you? What affirmed what you already know? List any thoughts and comments below so you can return to them at a later date:

Your
Greatest
Accomplishment

*"The things most important to us are also the things
we have to work hardest for."*

Take a moment to reflect back on your life and identify one of your greatest accomplishments. In other words, identify something personal of which you are most proud. What is it?

You might have several experiences or accomplishments; however, select the experience most significant and important to you.

Now, write this accomplishment below:

As you remember this accomplishment, ask yourself the following two questions:

Was this accomplishment a result from luck?

Was this accomplishment a result of something easy and overnight?

These are powerful questions because I strongly believe – and I would be willing to wager a complimentary keynote presentation – that what you identified involved sacrifice, hard work and dedication. I also believe that your greatest accomplishment was a direct result of significant, persistent effort over a long period of time. It was *not* a result of something easy or that simply happened to you overnight.

Am I correct?

If I am not correct, please let me know because you just earned a complimentary keynote!

Think about it. You have just realized one of the most important lessons of living a fulfilled life. Our greatest accomplishments do *not* result from luck. Rather, our proudest experiences are a result of us sacrificing for what we desire most and taking action persistently over a period of time.

The things most important to us are also the things we have to work the hardest for.

However, what does our fast-paced culture want us to think?

Our societal concepts of instant coffee and *instant success* portray an image that we should not necessarily have to work hard to achieve our dreams and that obstacles should be easy to overcome. Society makes most of us feel that if we encounter obstacles or setbacks, we are on the wrong track and will be criticized. We have become afraid of failure, and it's this fear of failure that usually is stronger than our desire for success!

However, this inaccurate assumption is backwards. It's wrong. By believing it, we get caught in the rat race of trying to live a fast-paced, easy and "safe" life void of failure and obstacles. It's impossible to live life this way.

"It is impossible to live without failing at something, unless you live so cautiously that you might as well not have lived at all, in which case you have failed by default."

~ J. K. Rowling

Fear is nothing but a state of mind, and it is the failure and setbacks we can learn the most from. Our mistakes serve as lessons of wisdom, but only when we ask ourselves the right questions. Sound familiar?

Even during an experience that is seemingly negative, frustrating, and appears to be a major setback, know that you are a better person as a result of it.

Think of your mind as a fertile soil and your thoughts as seeds being planted. When we allow bad thoughts to consume our minds, we are subconsciously planting bad seeds as well. And as a result, these bad seeds grow into large plants.

Bad seeds = Bad thoughts.

In contrast, what grows in your mind when you plant good thoughts? The results are that these good seeds grow in your mind and they become large plants as well.

Good seeds = Good thoughts.

Either way, your thinking is a result of what you focus on. And clearly with this example, you reap what you sow!

Remind yourself of your greatest accomplishments often, especially when you encounter obstacles and frustrations along the journey of pursuing your goal. The frustrations will will be there – expect them.

The power of your mental focus will dictate how you feel. And how you feel dictates how you act. So focus on the positive, even when it seems invisible, and you will find it. Again, learn from your past achievements because they can serve as lessons of wisdom. No one is ever defeated until they accept it as reality.

"Many of life's failures are people who did not realize how close they were to success when they gave up."
~ Thomas A. Edison

To watch my TEDx talk where I share my research and discovery about what all great leaders have in common, simply visit http://kevincsnyder.com/free-stuff ***(16 min)***

Before moving onto the next chapter, take a moment to reflect on how you feel right now. What did you learn from this chapter? What surprised you? What affirmed what you already know? <u>List any thoughts and comments below so you can return to them at a later date</u>:

The Power of Choice

"You are not <u>what</u> you think you are;

rather, what you <u>think</u>, you are."

~ Ancient Proverb

I had an incredible childhood, growing up in North Carolina with a brother, sister and two great, loving parents. I played sports, was good in school and was even active in the community volunteering at an early age.

I have a vivid memory of 6th grade, having lots of friends and "going with" several girls. When I was that age, "going with" was the precursor to dating. I felt like a rockstar.

6th grade was more fun than educational for me. My parents had to limit the number of phone calls I received at night and they ordered a second phone line just because I was on the phone, constantly. These were the days before cell phones!

In 7th grade, I dated "Crystal" and truly felt junior high lust for the first time. In fact, I liked Crystal so much that I wrote "I Love Crystal" on my blue Chucks shoes and on my desk in each class.

We had been dating for six months, which in 7th grade is equivalent to dog years, when one day she had a friend of hers break up with me in the cafeteria during lunch – in front of everyone. I was devastated and remember crying in front of all my friends. Obviously our breakup took me by surprise. I ran to the bathroom and stayed there for the entire lunch.

The next class period, I saw walking down the hallway holding hands with my best friend.

I charged him and felt like punching him to the ground. I could not believe it. Luckily, for both him and I, another friend held me back.

The next few days were painful. All I could think about was Crystal and why she broke up with me. I also constantly thought about my best friend and why he would do that to me as well.

I felt like I was not good enough for either of them. I remember wanting to be different for Crystal, more like my best friend, so that she might like me again. For the first time that I remember in my life, I faced rejection ... and this was only the beginning.

For the next several weeks, I faced even more rejection. My popularity seemed to diminish and phone calls at night almost stopped. All of a sudden I didn't feel like one of the coolest kids in school anymore. Moreover, I got cut during soccer team tryouts, a sport I loved and had played my entire life. I was really good at soccer so none of this made sense to me.

My life had changed suddenly and drastically, all outside of my control.

A few weeks later, I saw Crystal at a friend's birthday party. We eventually spoke later that evening. As we were talking she used her index finger to touch my stomach. Her exact words were, "Gaining a little bit of weight aren't we?" Her comment stuck to me and my mind kept repeating those words over and over.

Maybe if I lost some *weight*, she would like me again? Maybe if I lost some *weight*, I would be more popular again? Maybe my *weight* was a factor in me being cut from the soccer team?

I became convinced that my *weight* was the major source of rejection in all areas. It was to blame for everything.

Before I continue, I must acknowledge that I was not the thinnest kid in school nor was I the fattest. My pictures on the next page show I looked quite 'normal' like the average kid.

2nd *grade* 6th *grade*

Nevertheless, losing weight became a central focus point for me and I assumed it would help me gain control back in my life.

I didn't tell anyone, including my family, that I was going to lose weight. I started to diet but I just was not successful at it. I would eat the wrong foods at the wrong times and my focus was not a healthy lifestyle. For about six months, I went back and forth, losing and gaining about ten-fifteen pounds each time.

Since soccer didn't work out, I then tried out for the wrestling team. I was pretty good in my weight class of 110 lbs, but most of what I learned during that wrestling season was self-control and how to diet and control my weight. I mastered the ability to manage weight before wrestling matches by eating, not eating, exercising or not exercising. As a result, my weight consistently remained just under 110.

Then, just before the season was over, I decided to lose some more weight, hoping to look and feel better about myself. By this time, losing weight was something I knew I could accomplish.

I remember losing 5-10 lbs and feeling good. At this same time, I received compliments from people that I looked great. Crystal approached me one day and commented that I looked good. I associated my weight with everything - popularity, Crystal possibly liking me again and feeling good about myself in general.

I convinced myself that I needed to lose more weight in order to feel even better and get more attention. Losing weight became a drug and this is when my disordered behavior began. I would have Diet Coke for breakfast, skip dinner meals, exercise continuously at odd times of the day and night, isolate myself from friends around food, etc.

What started as dieting led into a preoccupation with food and exercise, which further led into destructive and unhealthy behavior, which led into self-esteem and body image problems, which ultimately led into my eating disorder.

The next several months were very dark as if my conscious thought shut down. I do not remember much other than exercising and drinking lots of diet soda and anything sugar free.

If I knew I had to be at family dinner, that would be the only meal I would eat all day. They of course would not know that. I would also run and exercise before my parents even woke up in the morning, usually at 5:00am. Running was followed by at least 500 sit-ups. This behavior and dark spiral progressively continued before anyone really knew what was going on, including me.

My mom told me a story several years ago where she first realized something was wrong. She recalled seeing me from a distance at church, yet not even recognizing me at first because I was so skinny. It was at that moment where she acknowledged I had lost too much weight. My mom and dad finally connected the dots.

During school that very next day, my mom secretly came to school and had me sent to the principal's office. I remember this vividly – it was 3rd period Algebra and the principal's secretary called my name over the intercom. All my classmates thought I was getting in trouble. I was shocked as well. What did I do?

I was surprised to see my mom when I arrived at the office. She was crying. She had come to take me to the doctor and assumed I would be extremely angry. Surprisingly enough though, I didn't say a word. I did notice a security officer around the corner.

Mom told me that we were going to the doctor because she was concerned. I didn't say a word. I just walked to the car with the security officer behind me. I'm confident he was instructed to ensure I wouldn't run away.

At the doctor, I weighed 76 lbs which was 29 lbs lighter than three months prior. My pulse was 49 beats/minute and the doctor was extremely worried.

The doctor asked if I had ever heard of "Anorexia Nervosa." I had not but it didn't sound good. I remember feeling so confused.

The doctor then informed my mother, with me standing next to her, that I had Anorexia Nervosa and needed to be admitted into a hospital immediately for treatment. The doctor emphatically stressed that my body could not lose another ounce and that if I did lose more weight, I was risking severe long-term complications, if not death.

Hearing this, I told my mom I was *not* going to some hospital. If I did, all my friends would know I had some sort of "problem." Ironically, all anyone had to do was look at me to know I was emaciated. As you'll see on the next page, I looked like a skeleton:

Below is picture of me the day before my mom took me to the doctor. It was our annual yearbook photo.

7th grade picture

While the doctor and my parents looked for hospitals and treatment centers, I was allowed to be at home as long as I gained weight and began counseling. This is when my battle started. I was forced to eat.

Being forced to gain weight was completely against the lifestyle I had developed. Even grasping the severity of my condition, I still did not recognize the importance of eating food – I was terrified of calories and the mental image of putting any "fat" back on my body was horrifying.

A few years ago, my dad informed me of a conversation he had with me during this dark time. He had asked me what it was about food that made me so scared. He said my response was:

*"Just being **near food** is like standing on the edge of a tank full of hungry sharks ... **eating food** is like being pushed in."*

My life continued to spiral out of control as I was forced to eat and begin the treatment process. Every day after school my mom would pick me up and take me to psychologists, psychiatrists, nutritionists, weird types of doctors, weigh-ins at the doctor's office, and other doctors that wanted to study my rare condition.

How my mother had time for this I still do not know, but she taxied me around every afternoon after school. We usually would not get home until right before dinner - this was my life for over six months. Doctors, doctors, weigh-ins, doctors ...

In the meantime, there were no hospitals available to me. There were eating disorder centers for females, but not males. There were clinics for adults but not adolescents. There were centers for juveniles with behavior and legal problems, but none were focused on eating disorders. Being a male, juvenile anorexic, my condition did not fit in any of these places, so I continued being treated while at home.

Again, I don't remember much during this dark time of my life. Maybe my subconscious did not want me to remember, or maybe my body and mind just shut down, like animals during hibernation.

For the first several weeks, my psychologist sessions were completely silent. I would sit there staring at the floor, feeling that the counselor was a waste of my time. I would not say a word and the counselor would let me sit there, occasionally asking me a question every fifteen minutes or so, hoping to spark some sort of conversation.

The weigh-ins at the doctor's office were even more difficult. After all, I was supposed to be gaining weight. If at any time my weight dropped, the doctor threatened to find a treatment facility in another state. I did not want that and I remember one time drinking nearly a full gallon of water just before a weigh-in. I knew I was a few pounds lighter that day and drinking that much water made my stomach almost burst. But I could not allow the doctor to catch me at a lighter weight.

One day, I broke down during one of my counseling sessions. I remember asking how long I would have to keep coming because all I wanted was to be "normal" again. I didn't feel normal coming to a psychologist – every time I went reminded me I had a problem. My psychologist didn't give me a direct answer but it was the first time she and I had actually spoken to her. I cried. I screamed at her. I hated being there.

While my mom was driving home that same day, I opened up the side door of the van going 65 mph and put one foot out, preparing to jump. I was so angry and out of control that I just wanted to end it all.

I heard my mom scream and she slammed on the brakes. I slammed against the front seat as the car came to an immediate stop.

That night I couldn't sleep. In fact, during this whole dark period I had clinical insomnia, sleeping maybe two or three hours a night. Routinely, I would go to bed near 10:00 or 11:00pm but my mind would be racing with all sorts of issues like exercising, foods to eat the next day, foods not to eat, fat on my body and how I was going to secretly exercise.

This one particular night changed everything though. My mom heard me crying in bed at about 2:00am. She walked into my room and sat down on my bed. I cried even more. After a few moments she said, "You're going to get better, honey. Please continue to be strong."

I cried for several more minutes. I finally said to her, "I can't go on like this. I hate my life. I just want to be normal again." We both cried for a few more minutes and then I fell asleep.

That particular day was the most important day of my life. I hit rock bottom. After finally yelling at my psychologist, nearly committing suicide and jumping out of a car on a busy highway, and emotionally breaking down with my mother, I woke up the next morning making a conscious *choice* to get healthy. And by finally making a decision to take back control of my life, I slowly began to heal.

I finally realized that I was not going to get better until I made the choice to do so.

The Power of Choice

I woke up the next morning feeling better than I had in months. I still did my normal routine of exercising before and after breakfast, but I felt motivated to get healthy again.

I still struggled with food, but I knew that gaining weight was the only way I could get back to a normal life. I changed my neuro-association with food, meaning I proactively changed my mental association of food from fear to being healthy and normal. Food was no longer the enemy – it was part of the equation to make me better.

Over the next several months, I gained about a ½ lb each week. I continued exercising, but at least I knew I was trying to put the weight back on in the right places. My doctor, counselor and parents were all OK with my workouts as long as I was gaining weight.

Once my weight rose to 86 lbs, I told the doctor I wanted to wrestle again. Even though he was proud of me for gaining 10 lbs, he denied my request. However, he and my mom both agreed that if I got to 95 lbs then I would have approval to join the wrestling team.

Gaining just enough weight, nine more lbs, to be back on the wrestling team became my goal. In fact, it became my obsession and I gained those remaining nine lbs in two weeks. I drank three 1,000 calorie protein shakes a day.

When I went back to the doctor two weeks later, he smiled. He was so proud of me. The doctor immediately wrote an approval note to my wrestling coach. I went to practice the next day and joined the 95 lb. pound weight class.

Three other guys were in the same weight class so I had to beat them in order to start on the team. Within the next week, I wrestled each of them during practice – and beat them all. I was the starter for the 95 lb weight class at the match the following week!

My mom and dad were extremely happy for me – they were also shocked. Even for me, this experience was surreal. I had set my goal to wrestle again and here I was better than ever. With all the exercise I had been doing, I was actually in perfect shape and I had gained the weight back in a healthy manner.

The next wrestling match was against our arch rival school. It was a big match and the gym was packed full of people. My mom and dad both came to see me perform.

To many people's surprise, including my own, I won my match! I didn't pin him but I did beat him by points. When I got off the wrestling mat, my coach hugged me and told me I had just beaten an undefeated wrestler and the previous year's conference champion!

The night before that day's match, the coach had called my parents and told them I was wrestling the best wrestler in the conference. He wanted my parents to be prepared because even he didn't expect me to win. They were all unsure how I would handle the defeat.

That season I dominated every remaining match, being undefeated and even winning the conference championship earning a gold medal. I even went further to the state competition and got third place in the state tournament.

Despite the negative press that wrestling often receives, wrestling gave me a positive focus. It was an activity I looked forward to each day. I truly believe wrestling distracted my focus from food and helped me work towards becoming a "normal" kid again.

We all need a positive focus.

My recovery continued to be an uphill battle but I recognized improvement each week. Some days were better than others but most days were good. My life finally seemed back in control.

As I got older, I wanted to forget this chapter of my life. Having anorexia was not an experience I was proud of. It wasn't until I began motivational speaking that I realized how my story could help others.

One of my favorite portions of each keynote presentation is talking to audience members afterward. I love hearing their stories and what messages best connected with them from my program. I have been amazed at how many people open up to me about their personal struggles and how often depression and addiction are common battles they have faced as well.

If I can serve one role for anyone, it is to prove to them that they are not alone. I believe my stories will help impact other's lives and will model a pathway towards healing, resilience and recovery. If I beat my disease, surely others can as well.

For those of you who might be struggling with an eating disorder, please talk with someone professional. I know how difficult it might be to reach out, but your life might depend on it. Make the choice to get better and become healthy. No one can do it for you, though. You may have to be like me and hit rock bottom first before you acknowledge the severity of your condition.

I was lucky – I got help before it was too late. Looking back, I was near death. If my mom had not taken me to the doctor that day during school, I might have died, or would at least have serious long-term health complications. I certainly would not have stopped the cycle myself. I was so depressed that I did not even recognize the dark depression I was in. My life had spiraled out of control.

However, my spiral was stopped because someone else stepped in. I eventually began the healing process once I made the conscious choice to accept help. I was reborn when I understood the power of choice. And I thank God that it was not too late.

For those of you who might someone who is struggling with anorexia, depression or any type of addiction, please help them. Show them you care. You might need to take action like my mom did for me. You'll likely need to try more than once. If you don't help them, who will?

As I mentioned before, I also believe that wrestling played a critical role in my recovery. To me it was more than just a sport. Wrestling was symbolic of the importance for goal setting. It was reflective of my desire to get healthy and I gave it 110%. When I conquered wrestling, I conquered anorexia. When I was awarded the gold medal at the conference tournament, I was awarded the gold medal for beating anorexia.

I am not a medical doctor and I am most certainly not a medical expert on eating disorders. However, I am an expert on the struggles I endured, my survival, my recovery and how I can make reason of my life experience.

I do not agree with the popular phrase, "Things happen for a reason." Rather, I prefer, "You have to make reason out of the things that happen."

Anorexia Nervosa, along with all eating disorders, is a serious mental disease – studies have found that complications from eating disorders kill up to nearly 20% of those diagnosed. Eating disorders are also the third most chronic illness amongst adolescent women.

People can and do recover from eating disorders. If you or someone you know is struggling with anorexia, help them. Talk to them and do all you can to get them professional help. The longer the symptoms are ignored or denied, the more difficult recovery will be.

For more information about identifying eating disorders, prevention and how you can help, please visit:

www.mentalhealth.samhsa.gov

www.nami.org

www.emedicinehealth.com

www.edreferral.com

Healthy bodies come in all shapes and sizes. We don't need to change our bodies, we need to change our attitudes.

Before moving onto the next chapter, take a moment to reflect on how you feel right now. What did you learn from this chapter? What surprised you? What affirmed what you already know? <u>List any thoughts and comments below so you can return to them at a later date</u>:

The Secret

"Imagination is the preview to life's coming attractions."

~ Albert Einstein

Have you heard of the phenomena called *The Secret*? It's a concept that bloomed in the mid-2000s and was both a film and book. *The Secret* was so successful that many experts were already projecting it to be the most successful personal development program in history.

To watch "The Secret" inspirational movie clip, simply visit
http://kevincsnyder.com/free-stuff ***(6 min)***

Still intrigued to know what *The Secret* is? I wish I could share it with you but unfortunately I can't, because after all, it's a secret.

Actually, not only will I share with you some of the philosophy explained in *The Secret*, I will share more. I will introduce my interpretation of how it will change your life once it is understood and applied.

What is *The Secret*?

The author of *The Secret*, Rhonda Byrne, has based its concept primarily upon the Law of Attraction, which she describes as a universal law suggesting that *like attracts like*. Everything in the world, or universe as she describes, is comprised of energy and this energy attracts *like* energy. For example, as we think good thoughts and feel good, we resultantly attract more of these good things into our lives.

The same result happens when we think and focus on negative thoughts and feelings; we attract more of these negative circumstances into our lives as well. So in its simplicity, *The Secret* says you get what you focus on, good or bad. Sound familiar?

The Secret has people talking, as if it were a discovery just found in a deep abyss. In reality, though, its principles can also be found in most teachings of any past or present inspirational speaker, success coach or motivational author including yours truly. For example, Anthony Robbins, Norman Vincent Peale, Wayne Dyer, and Zig Ziglar all have expressed and taught a concurring belief system that explains (1) when we know what we want, (2) are focused, committed, and passionate about it truly happening, (3) take persistent action toward this goal, (4) then we will manifest our desires.

Principals from *The Secret* can also be found in the *Bible*. Books that The Secret do give credit to for being an influence include *As a Man Thinketh* and *Think and Grow Rich,* both of whom I have previously credited throughout this book.

So as you might be able to sense from my interpretation of *The Secret*, I do not consider this philosophy such a secret. However, I do validate its intentional, *brilliantly marketed,* and well-articulated message that challenges us to awaken and bring about the personal power that already lies within each of us. Its concept is much more than positive thinking; it is positive *believing.*

"Our brains become magnetized with the dominating thoughts which we hold in our minds. These "magnets" attract to us the forces, the people, the circumstances of life which harmonize with the nature of our dominating thoughts."

~ Napolean Hill, *Think and Grow Rich*

Applying *The Secret*

It might be hard to agree with or understand, but the philosophy shared in *The Secret* should challenge each of us to identify and awaken forgotten dreams and goals we have not pursued or believed possible. Our greatest dreams cannot manifest in our life until we invite them. Remember your proudest accomplishment? Did this happen by accident or was it a result of your belief and persistent action? You already know *The Secret* whether you realize it or not!

Identify a personal or professional goal and desire you are passionate about and have this goal be as extreme and ridiculous as you can possibly imagine. This has to be a goal you truly desire and more importantly, a goal you truly believe in and are passionate about. Do not focus on "how" you will manifest this goal in your life. The "how" will show up, but only *if* you truly believe in it first.

As I paraphrase what *Chicken Soup for the Soul* co-author Jack Canfield says in *The Secret*, you should equate the "how" of your goals with driving your car during the night. When you drive at night, your headlights only show you 200 feet in front of the car. Yet you can drive from California to New York by only seeing every 200 feet, as long as you have faith to continue driving.

Again, do not focus on or wait for the plan or "how" to achieve your identified goal, the "how" will become more clear as you focus on it, believe in it and take those first steps toward pursuing it. Your subconscious and conscious mind will bring it to you.

Write your desire below.

Now that you have identified what your goal is, begin to visualize yourself already accomplishing and receiving it. Focus on it already in your life.

Close your eyes and actually visualize this goal and desire in your life. See it clearly in your mind with specific detail. If it's financial, how much exactly and by when exactly? If it's a tangible product, what color is it? If it's relationship oriented, describe it in great detail to yourself.

Just as the Law of Attraction promises, you will begin to attract this outcome like a magnet and manifest in your life. That is, if you completed the activity with clarity and detail and you truly, truly envision it in your life. It cannot be a vision you *hope* happens. You must envision it knowing it *will* manifest. There's a crucial difference between *hope* and *expectancy*. True or true?

This is the part of dream visualization that most people do not understand. They must envision and expect. Because they do not understand it, they never attract its full potential to their life.

From the previous page, if you have visualized your desire correctly and without distraction, your chest should be full of energy right now. If you do not feel this, then revisit the previous page and repeat the activity. This energy is the emotion and state of mind you must capture as you begin to take action toward this goal. Remember, like attracts like!

Try this exercise repeatedly in a setting where you can truly focus. Results may or may not happen overnight, but you will feel and see progress eventually. Then repeat this exercise with every desire you identify.

As we utilize our ability to intentionally focus on unwavering success and continually improving upon what works well, we become incredibly powerful. Our energy becomes magnetic and attracts positive circumstances. We exercise the personal power within our mind and manifest the goals in our personal and professional lives.

<u>Disclaimer</u>:
The law of attraction only works for people who believe it will!

Before moving onto the next chapter, take a moment to reflect on how you feel right now. What did you learn from this chapter? What surprised you? What affirmed what you already know? <u>List any thoughts and comments below so you can return to them at a later date</u>:

More to
The Secret

"*What you're thinking is what you're becoming.*"

~ Muhammed Ali

As often as I share the philosophy behind *The Secret*, I am routinely confronted by people who say it will not work, that it is un-Christian and that it is unrealistic and naïve to believe you can literally attract circumstances in your life. In response to them, I usually just smile and agree with them.

Note: see disclaimer at end of previous chapter!

Sometimes I will share with them an extraordinary story of when I put *The Secret* to the test and why I am so dedicated to now live by its principles on a daily basis. Before my test, I had doubts about the Law of Attraction myself. I felt, and still do feel, that persistent action is required to achieve goals and dreams, in addition to believing in passionate goals and envisioning success.

Contrary to what the *The Secret* suggested, you cannot just sit back, dream big thoughts about a Ferrari, and expect a Ferrari to be outside in your driveway. Just doing that is unrealistic, lazy and simply naïve.

Many people live by *The Secret* but just don't know it – remember *The Secret* really is not a secret. It has just been brilliantly packaged so anyone can understand and learn from it. Even when Oprah Winfrey had several of the main philosophers on her show several years ago, she admitted that she had always lived by the same philosophy they were sharing, but that she did not call it a secret!

I felt, and feel, the exact same way, but I never acknowledged the importance of being even more focused on the visualization process for achieving my goals. Meaning, I never recognized that perhaps the "thought" process was just as important as the "action" process. That the equation for achieving extreme levels of success was based on these two factors, interdependently.

"Anything the mind can believe, it can conceive."

~Thomas Edison

"All goals in life must first begin with a dream."

~ Walt Disney

"Nothing will change in your life until you make a change about how you think about it."

~ Wayne Dyer

Think about my *Price is Right* story (Chapter 2). Before I ever met Bob Barker and was a contestant on the show, I knew without any doubt, that I would be shaking hands with him on stage, specifically on national television! I had a mental image so strongly vivid that I envisioned myself with him before it ever happened. Was it luck that I actually did get called down to contestants row? Or perhaps was it the Law of Attraction at work in my life?

I lived my dream despite hurdles and obstacles along the way. But as I remembered this experience, it struck me that perhaps something greater than me was at work to manifest that reality in my life. With *The Secret* fresh in my mind, I decided to create a Vision Board and set a few more goals that were just as extreme, if not more so, than my dream of being on *The Price is Right*!

The Secret introduces the powerful concept of a Vision Board, which is literally visual imagery with your desires, goals, declarations and dreams. It is symbolic of what you truly want in your life, and what you passionately believe you are attracting to you. It could be in the form of a board, i.e. Vision Board, but also a sheet of paper, a computer screensaver, etc. It's whatever you decide for it to be.

My Vision Board was, and still is, very simple. When I made my first board, I had clippings of items from magazines and phrases I typed myself, all cut and pasted onto a fluorescent orange poster board. My board was reflective of my true desires and was comprised of things I honestly saw myself achieving. That is Rule #1 with your Vision Board; you must passionately believe in everything you put on there. You can't post goals you don't actually envision manifesting. That's why it's called a Vision Board, not a Hope Board.

On my Vision Board, just some of the items I put on there were a job promotion, the date for that new job ,the salary I was going to make in that new job, a partnership with a speakers bureau, acceptance into a doctoral program, completion for that doctorate degree with a date, a doctorate degree "paid for," a dog leash invention, and <u>this book</u>.

Again, it is essential that you realize my goals were truly "visions" at the time I put them on my Vision Board. I believed in them and saw them in my life but they were only dreams in my mind. And some of them, quite frankly, were ridiculous. I had no clue "how" they were going to arrive into my life, but I believed that they would.

Note: see disclaimer at end of previous chapter once again!

Within one year of making that first Vision Board, read what happened ...

Not only did I (1) accept a new dream job, (2) receive a salary within $1,000 of what was on my Vision Board, but (3) I became a professional speaker with CAMPUSPEAK, (4) was admitted into a doctorate program and (5) I was approached by the Vice President of my university telling me that my doctorate program would be "paid for" if I took my promotion. Are you freakin' kidding me?!

So my "test" to see if the Vision Board concept truly worked proved true to me several years ago. It was actually fun to play around and treat this concept like yet another game I knew I would win.

But I am not done yet – the best example is still to come.

For years, I had an idea about a dog leash invention. When my dogs were puppies, a lab named Guinness and an English bulldog named Snuka, I would take them for walks only to be frustrated that their leash lines would consistently become tangled. I would spend nearly half the time during our walks untangling their leash lines.

I began shopping around for a dual, retractable leash that would solve my problem. Unfortunately, I could not find a retractable product out on the market designed for walking two dogs. I went to all the retail pet stores, veterinarians, online stores and more. But I found nothing close to my idea.

Then, the idea hit me to <u>invent</u> the product I was looking for.

I started my invention adventure by doing research on the concept of multi-dog pet leashes. I spent countless hours on the Internet and visiting pet stores, trying to determine if my pet leash product already existed. After nearly clicking to end of the Internet and traveling over two hundred miles, I felt confident that my idea did *not* exist. I could not find any products even comparable.

But even though my idea was crystal clear in thought, I had no clue how to actually make it. I mentally envisioned the leash functioning and walking two dogs simultaneously, but I was absolutely lost when I attempted to describe the component parts that made the leash actually work. The "how" of my leash concept was the obstacle I could not overcome. I became very frustrated.

As a result, my invention was put on hold. Six months later, my idea was still on hold. And even though I thought about it frequently, all I did was *think*! I could never figure out how to actually make the leash. The frustration would always return. Again, the "how" of my idea got in the way.

Looking back, I also had focused my energy on *not* knowing how to create it, rather than attracting the circumstances to get it created. If only I understood the power of the Law of Attraction then.

One year went by. Then two. Then another. No leash. I always had excuses explaining why the leash would *not* work – I was too busy, patents are too expensive, I do not know how to make it, etc. I was more creative with finding excuses than I was with identifying solutions to my problems. Sound familiar?

But when I created my Vision Board, things changed drastically. Four years after conceiving the leash idea, I made the choice to re-kindle my efforts and pursue the leash idea once again. The difference this time though, was *action* and my focus shifted from reasons why I couldn't make it, to reasons why I could.

With the Law of Attraction fresh in my mind, all my mental energy focused on the invention and creation of the leash. I removed all doubt and all excuses that had been holding me back.

Exactly six days after pasting the phrase, "The No-Tangle! Multi-Retractable Dog Leash," on my Vision Board, a student of mine, (Mike) walked up to me and literally asked if

I had ever wanted to invent something. I smiled in utter disbelief.

I asked Mike what he was interested in inventing. He replied, saying he didn't have an idea, but that he felt I might.

After a few more questions, it turns out that Mike was one of the best computer design students at the university. He was also an engineering physics major, which means he had the brains and computer skills I had been needing since my invention conception. He was the "how" of my dream.

That very next weekend, Mike and I met. I brought several single retractable leashes with me, just so we could break them apart and study how they were designed.

To my amazement, within 45 minutes we had drafted the leash concept I had envisioned and dreamed about. For four years I procrastinated but in less than one hour it became a reality. Mike was the missing link that arrived as soon as I decided to put the leash on the Vision Board and committed to the idea.

The story continues ...

The very next weekend, I was at a nearby restaurant with some friends. I was introduced to someone to whom I felt an immediate energy and connection with. After talking with her for several minutes, I asked her what type of profession she was in. She replied, "I am a distributor for pet supplies."

I almost fainted. She had no clue I had just invented a newly-designed dog leash. Once Mike and I created the leash, she would be the distributor to help us sell it.

Two weeks after meeting her, I received a phone message from a friend who is a flight attendant calling to offer me her "Buddy Pass," which means I can fly stand-by for free, anywhere her airline flies. And when I need to travel to exhibit my dog leash to executives and companies interested in licensing it, I can fly for free.

Again, I could not believe how all this was happening to me. It was as if red carpet was being laid out before my eyes, showing me the way to manifest the leash and become amazingly successful.

"Imagination will often carry us to worlds that never were. But without it we go nowhere."

~ Carl Sagan, American Astronomer and Astrochemist

After four years, I finally made the conscious choice not just to "try" and create the leash, but rather, I made the decision that I would create the leash. I put my focus on the creation of it, versus "how" I was going to create it. And when my focus was clear, so was the path made for me.

I met Mike, then my new pet product distributor friend, then the flight attendant. How did this all happen? Was it coincidence? Was it luck? The Law of Attraction at work?

This leash story is just another surreal and exciting example of how you can make anything happen in your life, as long as you believe in it enough, are passionate enough, and willing to make the choice to see it through.

Interested in seeing what the No-Tangle looks like?
Simply do a Google search for *Freedom Leash*™
and you'll be amazed.

It is simple to create your own Vision Board. What I first want you to do is think of all the things you desire out of life. What is it you are seeking? What is it that would truly make you feel fulfilled? What are your goals? Where do you see yourself in one year? Five years? Ten years? What does you future spouse look like? Your home? Your bank account?

You must be as specific as possible.

Identify and focus on your desires. List everything you want in your life right now on the next page:

VISION BOARD

(Write whatever comes to your mind. Please trust this process.)

I assume you have written items on your Vision Board this time! But before we continue, I must stress to you that the items you listed must be goals you believe in and are passionate about. They do not have to be realistic; in fact, I would hope some of them seem ridiculous! However, it is imperative that you believe in them so strongly that you already visualize them in your mind.

"There is a difference between wishing for something and being ready to receive it. No one is ready until they believe they can actually acquire it. The state of mind must be belief."

~ As a Man Thinketh

Remember, Thomas Edison dreamed of a lamp operated by electricity before he created it. When he put his dream to action, despite 10,000 failures, he persisted until he made it a physical reality! The Wright brothers dreamed of a machine that would fly through the air and despite hundreds of unsuccessful attempts, they finally achieved flight!

You have to be convinced that it is only a matter of time before these items tangibly in your life. If you do not feel this strongly about items on your Vision Board, either believe more strongly in them, or remove them from your Board. The Board will only work if you vision these items specifically in your mind first!

Remember, what you think about you bring about!

Congratulations! You have just created your first Vision Board! Now either photocopy or rip this Vision Board page out of the book and place it proudly in an area where you will see it daily. This will serve as a reminder to you that you must continue to focus on and make efforts towards achieving the goals you have listed.

However, you cannot just sit back and expect these goals to manifest in your life. As I've hinted earlier in this chapter, this is where I emphatically disagree with some philosophers when they describe the Law of Attraction. For this law to work, and for your Vision Board to create abundance for you, your passion for these things must be so strong that it *compels you to take action*. And as you begin making efforts, opportunities and doors will begin opening up for you in areas that you have never seen before.

I would rather be ready for an opportunity and not have one, than to have an opportunity and not be ready.

Remember my Vision Board? I was passionate about everything listed and opportunities arose where I never even imagined. It was synergetic and like magic! I wish for you the same!

I am proud of you for completing what is most likely your first Vision Board (or at least I hope you did). This was a crucial step for you to begin "playing" with this mentality and approach in life. But this Vision Board is only a "baby" board.

Now, or when you are ready, I want you to make another version that is HUGE! I want you to go buy poster board and cut out phrases and clippings from magazines and newspapers that reflect these same messages on your baby board. You need something you can display with pride! Spend more time creating it than what you did earlier. Be proud of your board - there are no limitations except those we focus on. You can create anything which you can imagine.

I have shared a great deal of information with you in this chapter, and perhaps it is overwhelming. Truthfully, I hope it has been! I hope you are feeling challenged. Because challenges breed change and change breeds growth.

I want you to believe in your goals as much as I do. I want you to feel as fulfilled as I do. I want you to capture this power of your mental focus as much as I have and I want you to do something with it. Self-mastery is the hardest job you will ever tackle. Once you understand and believe that it works, I want you to it teach someone else.

Before moving onto the next chapter, take a moment to reflect on how you feel right now. What did you learn from this chapter? What surprised you? What affirmed what you already know? <u>List any thoughts and comments below so you can return to them at a later date</u>:

Mastering the Art of Effective Communication

"We have two ears and one mouth for a reason."

Communication is the foundation for both success and failure. Research from Fortune 500 companies, CEO's, business owners, and entrepreneurs all support that effective communication is essential. They also share that poor communication is the root of all organizational breakdown.

Communication experts say that roughly 90% percent of communication is nonverbal. Meaning, only ten percent of our communication is actually spoken. If this is the case, then what makes up the ninety percent?

"How" we communicate says so much more than what words come from our mouth. It is our body language when we speak, our facial expressions, the tone in our voice, our posture, our smile, and more. Each of these non-verbal gestures sends and perpetuates a clear message before our words are even heard or understood.

It's not what you say, it's how you say it.

Yet most ineffective communicators do not understand this, let alone utilize this to their advantage. When poor communicators need to communicate, they often do so without understanding that their own body language, vocal tone and facial expressions are saying so much more. Often times, simply smiling and having effective body language says more than someone's mouth.

Are you aware of your body language? Were you thinking about body language last time you made a presentation or had to confront a friend? What about your next upcoming presentation or group meeting – will you remember the importance of keeping good eye contact, facial expressions, and posture? Again, remember that 90% of what you say is not even communicated in words; a message is sent by "how" you say it.

The most important thing in communication is to hear what isn't being said.

Most of communication in today's fast-paced society is unspoken, not only because of body language, but also because of technology.

Think for a moment about all the ways you communicate on a daily basis. How often do you write a letter and send it in the mail? I would assume it has been a while, if you can even remember. In fact, the last envelope most people have "snail mailed" was a bill they were paying with check!

Snail mail has been replaced by a plethora of other available communication strategies such as email, text messaging, Facebook, Twitter, LinkedIn, Instagram, other various social media and app platforms, etc. Think of all the ways you have communicated today alone. Chances are you have utilized several of the methods listed above.

The important concept I want you to acknowledge is that our communication has evolved from less face-to-face conversations to more electronic. At times, it seems we do not even need face-to-face interactions because everything can be "spoken" electronically. This has made communication more easy and immediate, but has it made communication more effective?

The more we rely on technology to get our message across, the more we "think" we have communicated. However, just because we send an email or a message on Facebook, does that truly ensure effective communication?   Of course not.

We have all sent and read emails that become misinterpreted. We have all sent and read emails whose message would have been different if it were spoken face-to-face. Across classrooms, in residence halls, in our homes, and in our offices, we routinely text or instant message someone next door, in the next cubicle, or even our own room!

To be effective communicators we must understand that just because we send a message, such as an email, it does not mean we have "communicated." We cannot rely on technology to substitute for conversations that should be taking place in person. We think we have communicated – but we have not.

The single biggest problem in communication is the illusion that it has taken place.

Have you heard, or even said, any of the following:

You didn't get my email?
We posted the minutes. You didn't read them?
We sent everyone a message on Facebook.
Your message must have gone to my SPAM.
Our email was down for the day.
You didn't get my text?

Above are just some of the excuses people commonly share for not receiving messages. I have heard every one of them ... I've given a few myself. Sometimes they are honest; sometimes they are nice little white lies because we know we can blame technology. It frequently doesn't work, yet we rely on it so much.

We depend upon technology so much that we have become passive communicators. We send an email and think it's done, that the issue is handled. The major problem with this approach is that you can never be sure when or if the person actually received the message. There is no reply until it is too late or after a decision has already been made.

So the next time you have something very important to communicate, why not utilize several strategies to ensure the message gets across. More importantly, why not call the person directly? If its business, why not arrange a meeting? Meetings can be 5-10 minutes and short. My rule of thumb is:

If I need to scroll to read it, I pick up the phone.

Remember, just because you think you have communicated does not mean you actually have. Your message could have easily gotten lost in process or it could have just as easily never been sent. And when you are face-to-face, do not forget the messages you send by not speaking at all.

Remember, it's not what you say, but how you say it!

Note: My most requested workshop is titled, "High Performance Communication!" and you can download the PowerPoint and handouts via my website, www.KevinCSnyder.com/Resources or you can find it on www.SlideShare.com by searching for "Kevin Snyder and High Performance Communication."

Gratitude

"Nothing new can come in your life until
you appreciate what you already have."
~ Michael Beckwith

At the closing of every presentation, I share the following message and give out rocks, which I call my "Gratitude Rocks." Even though you may not have a "Gratitude Rock" with you this moment, I want you to immediately identify something near you that is both tangible and special. Find something that is symbolic to you.

Once you have the item, read the following:

> *Keep this item in a special place, so that every time you see it or touch it, you will be reminded of the many things in your life you can be grateful for. You cannot attract any more into your life until you appreciate what you already have.*

Focus on living in abundance and you will attract more of it, because you are powerfully attracting more good things to you. It's the Law of Attraction – you become what you think about most; by your thinking, you attract!

The greatest teachers and inventors who have ever lived have told us that the Law of Attraction is the most powerful law. What you focus on, you attract to you. This Law responds to your thoughts, both positive and negative. Most people think and focus on what they do *not* want, like problems and debt, for example. Then they wonder why these things keep showing up in their lives over and over again. But when you focus on what you want, what you do not want will go away.

When you become aware of this great law, you become aware of how incredibly powerful you are.

You have the magnetic power to change anything in your life, because you are the one who chooses your thoughts.

It is a well-known fact that one believes whatever one repeats to one's self, whether the statement is true or false. We are what we are because of the dominating thoughts which we *permit* to occupy our mind!

If you can think it in your mind, you will manifest it in your life. You have the power to change your life by changing your thoughts and feelings. This is your life, and it's been waiting for you to discover it. You deserve all the good things life has to offer.

"If you think you'll lose, you're lost
For out of the world we find,
Success begins with a fellow's will.
It's all in the state of mind.

Life's battles don't always go
To the stronger or faster man,
But soon or late the man who win's
Is the one WHO THINKS HE CAN!"

~ Napolean Hill, *Think and Grow Rich*

The Essence
of Survival

Every morning in Africa, a lion wakes up. It knows it must run faster than the slowest gazelle, or else it will starve to death.

Every morning in Africa, a gazelle wakes up. It knows it must run faster than the slowest lion or else it will be eaten.

In Africa, it doesn't matter whether you are a lion or gazelle, because the when the sun comes up, you'd better be running.

———————————————————————

This book is about you. This book is about *thinking differently* than most people, and by *thinking differently* you will become magnificently successful and fulfilled. This book is also about identifying the role you choose to play in your own life.

Will you be a lion or will you be a gazelle?

You could be the youngest freshman at a university or rather you could be the Homecoming King/Queen.

You could be the president of an organization or rather you could be that common member holding no official position.

You could be the president/CEO of your own company or you could be an incredible office manager who shows up and does good work.

You could be a school principal or district superintendent or you could be a caring math teacher like my mom and sister.

Regardless of position, what role will you play in your own life? That's what you have to figure out.

Every one of us has something in our life we would like to see different or changed. For that change to begin though, we must realize we have a role in making that change. Change is a result of action. It's a result of thinking differently. It's a result of taking action and recognizing the role we have ... in everything.

Leadership is about <u>action</u>, not position. Leadership is about <u>transformation</u>, not transaction. Leadership is about <u>influence</u>, not management. Leadership is also a <u>verb</u>, not a noun.

~ Kevin Snyder

Every chapter you have read in this book has a message of personal power. The common denominator theme is that passion, commitment, sacrifice, and an unwavering positive attitude can attract everything you want in life.

You deserve everything you have the courage to ask for.

Think differently.

A Wish For Leaders

I sincerely wish you will all have the experience of thinking up a new idea, planning it, organizing it, and following it to completion, and then have it be magnificently successful.

I also hope you'll go through the same process and then have something "bomb out."

I wish you could know how it feels "to run" with all your heart and lose...horribly.

I wish that you could achieve some great good for mankind but have nobody know about it except you.

I wish you could find something so worthwhile that you deem it worthy of investing your life within it.

I hope you become frustrated and challenged enough to begin to push back the very barriers of your own personal limitations.

I hope you make a stupid mistake and get caught red-handed and are big enough to say those magic words: "I was wrong."

I hope you give so much of yourself that some days you wonder, "Is it worth all the effort?"

I wish for you a magnificent obsession that will give you reason for living and purpose and direction and life.

I wish for you the worst kind of criticism for everything you do, because that makes you fight to achieve beyond what you normally would.

I wish for you

the experience of leadership.

Motivation Matters!

I would love to stay in touch!

Subscribe to my motivational e-newsletter and receive a

weekly motivational message or my "Daily Dose" notification!

Simply visit www.KevinCSnyder.com
to subscribe! Receive your "Daily
Dose" of inspiration by downloading
my leadership app!

KevinCSnyder

Follow me on your social of choice
@KevinCSnyder

DIAMONDS ARE ONLY MADE
BY PRESSURE

Do you know how diamonds are actually formed? Read this- it will change your perception:

The very word diamond is derived from the Greek word *adamos*, meaning the unconquerable. It is known as one of the strongest and most chemically inert materials known. The diamond is nearly impossible to break & can nearly withstand the attack of any chemical. Interestingly, natural diamonds are produced deep under the Earth's crust under conditions of high temperature and high pressure.

This story explaining the creation of the diamond should remind us how life's pressure can make us stronger, more beautiful people. We cannot produce diamonds without first understanding our own natural qualities and overcoming life's frustrations. The pressure we experience also creates who are, and who we will become.

Perhaps there is a diamond of opportunity hidden in that difficulty you're experiencing now. It may not become a diamond just yet, but be patient, it is forming within you. The diamond scratches all and is not scratched by any.

QUOTES

*"Somebody is always doing
what somebody else said couldn't be done."*
~ Author Unknown

*"In the middle of every difficulty lies opportunity - once
discovered, such opportunities are like valuable diamonds
hidden in the sand."*
~ Albert Einstein

*"When we long for life without difficulties,
remind us that oaks grow strong in contrary winds and
diamonds are made under pressure."*
~ Author Unknown

"Try to be a rainbow in someone's cloud."
~ Maya Angelou

THE SEVEN UP'S

1. Wake Up! Decide to have a good day.

2. Dress Up! The best way to dress up is to put on a smile. A smile is an inexpensive way to improve your looks.

3. Shut Up! Say nice things and learn to listen. We have two ears and one mouth for a reason.

4. Stand Up! For what you believe in. Stand for something or you will fall for anything.

5. Look Up! To the Lord, higher power and universe you believe in.

6. Reach Up! For your goals, dreams and aspirations. Expect you will achieve them.

7. Lift Up! Be grateful for what you DO have. Nothing new can come into your life until you appreciate what you already have.

What do you wake up for, dress up for, stand up for, look up toward and lift up?

THE POWER TO REALLY LIVE

I like what Mark Twain said about enthusiasm. When asked the reason for his success, he replied, "I was born excited."

The happiest, most fulfilled and most successful people have discovered the necessity of an enthusiastic approach to living. Thomas Edison was also such a person. He was known for his energy and verve. He eventually acquired 1,093 patents for his inventions, including the electric light bulb, phonograph and motion picture camera. He was known to work tirelessly and joyfully. He seemed to love what he did and pursued it with passion. Others have made more money than Thomas Edison, but none have been more enthusiastic or productive.

Ralph Waldo Emerson once said, "Enthusiasm is one of the most powerful engines of success. When you do a thing, do it with all your might. Put your whole soul into it. Stamp it with your own personality. Be active, be energetic, be enthusiastic and faithful, and you will accomplish your object." Enthusiasm is an engine fueled by a love for what we do. It will power us anywhere we want to go and take us places we would never reach without it!

What are you enthusiastic about? What do you desire?

ACHIEVING YOUR DREAMS

"It's not what you are that holds you back.
It's what you think you're not."
~ Denis Waitley

Those wise words from Denis Waitley probably explain more people's failure to achieve the life they seek than any other quote I'm aware of. What keeps most people from achieving their dreams is that they spend too much time dwelling on their weaknesses and shortcomings instead of focusing on their gifts. And that's significantly due to their self-esteem, or lack thereof. Remember, you get what you focus on. And what you focus on expands.

QUOTES

"Happiest are the people who give most happiness to others."
~ Dennis Diderot, Philosopher

"Start by doing what's necessary; then do what's possible; and suddenly you are doing the impossible."
~ Francis of Assisi

"No one has a right to consume happiness without producing it."
~ Helen Keller, American author and lecturer

"What would you do differently if you knew you could not fail?"
~ Robert H. Schuller

THE POWER OF GIVING

Ever heard this before: "I gave away what I had, to get what I wanted"? It is so true. But you see, most people focus on the "get." I need to "get this," to "get that" … no, no, no. That's the hard way, the slow way. The way to GET is to GIVE. Success in our lives and profession is about service and giving to others. Whatever you want more of, start to give it away.

You want more time? Volunteer.

You want better knowledge? Give away some books.

You want better relationships? Be a great friend.

Want more money? Donate money to someone who really needs it.

What you sow, you'll reap. What does a farmer do? He plants a seed and a harvest is created. Take an inventory of what you have to give away. What about a smile, insight, time, or money. Stop holding on tight and start opening up and putting yourself in the FLOW of life - giving and receiving. It makes the world go round.

What are your talents, gifts and skills? How do you share them? Do you "give" them away?

HAPPINESS

Happiness can be caught, sought or thought, but never bought. The best way to keep happiness is to share it. Happiness is not created by what happens to us, but by our attitudes toward each happening. It isn't our position but our disposition which makes us happy. Stopping at third base adds nothing to the score. That lucky rabbit's foot didn't work for the rabbit. Even a woodpecker owes his success to the fact that he uses his head.

Anywhere is paradise; it's up to you. Happiness is a slice of life - buttered. If you think you can or you think you can't, you're right!

<u>QUOTES</u>

"If you want happiness for an hour - take a nap.
If you want happiness for a day - go fishing.
If you want happiness for a year - inherit a fortune.
If you want happiness for a lifetime - help someone else."
~ Chinese Proverb

"You don't have to get it right, you just have to get it going."
~ Mike Litman

"The more you seek security, the less of it you have. But the
more you seek opportunity, the more likely it is that you will
achieve the security that you desire."
~ Brian Tracy

THE ROAD TO SUCCESS
IS NOT STRAIGHT

There is a curve called Failure, a loop called Confusion, speed bumps called Friends, red lights called Enemies, exits called Temptation, caution lights called Family & possibly flat tires called Jobs.

But if you have a spare tire called Determination, an engine called Persistence, a map called Passion, insurance called Faith, a driver called Creator, you will arrive at your destination called SUCCESS!

Everybody, Somebody, Anybody & Nobody

This is a little story about four people named Everybody, Somebody, Anybody, and Nobody.

There was an important job to be done and Everybody was sure that Somebody would do it.

Anybody could have done it, but Nobody did it.

Somebody got angry about that because it was Everybody's job.

Everybody thought that Anybody could do it, but Nobody realized that Everybody wouldn't do it.

It ended up that Everybody blamed Somebody when Nobody did what Anybody could have done.

A bit more about the author, Kevin Snyder

Dr. Kevin Snyder is a motivational speaker and author with a PASSION for helping individuals and organizations empower themselves and others.

Through his motivational speaking career, Kevin has presented for over 500,000 people, over 1,150 audiences in all 50 states and numerous countries.

A selection of corporate and professional groups below:

A selection of school and college/university groups below:

Kevin speaks to high schools, colleges, professional organizations and associations of all types. He is the Founder of *Empower YOUth!* which is a 'menu' of inspirational youth keynotes customized for school assemblies, teacher in-service events, district personnel trainings, leadership conferences, parent events and more! To learn more, please visit Kevin's website and click on the "Keynote Programs" tab.

DYNAMIC LEADERSHIP PRESENTATIONS FOR STUDENTS AND EDUCATORS

Kevin has taught at the high school, community college and university level. Prior to becoming a professional speaker, Kevin held a career in Student Affairs and most recently served as the Dean of Students for High Point University. Prior to HPU, he served the University of Central Florida as the Director for the College of Education. He also worked at Embry-Riddle Aeronautical University and the University of South Carolina. Kevin's Masters and Doctorate degrees are both in Educational Leadership.

To learn more about any of Kevin's presentations, please visit his website and click on the "Keynote Programs" tab.

www.KevinCSnyder.com

Are you interested in speaking?

Curious what it takes to become a professional speaker?

I've written a book where I share it all!

Purchase
How to Become a Professional Speaker: PAID To SPEAK!
via Amazon

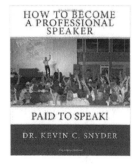

I also encourage you to visit my "Coaching" tab

on my website by visiting:

http://kevincsnyder.com/speakerauthor-coaching

Are you interested in writing a book?

Curious what it takes to become a published author?

Download your FREE eBook, "*How to Write a Book in 90 Days!*"

Simply visit
www.WriteWayPublishingCompany.com

Tell us more about your book concept and we'll tell you exactly what you need to do in order to get it published!

Let me send you a special link to download my other leadership books for FREE!

Thank you for investing your valuable time to read *Think Differently*! Since we're of "like mind," I'd like to send you a special link that offers my other leadership books as free eBook downloads. Simply visit www.KevinCSnyder.com and enter your email. You'll receive an immediate response with the special link.

Also, while reading or anytime afterwards, send me a message any way you like – through email, social media, website, etc. Share your thoughts, your struggles and your new-found strengths. I'd be honored to hear from you.

After you finish reading, share a testimonial! I'd love to read your thoughts which will help spread this positive message to others. Submit your testimonial on Amazon.com by following these easy steps:

#1: Visit www.Amazon.com

#2: In the Amazon search bar, type "Think Differently and Kevin Snyder" so that you find this book. Click on it!

#3: Then scroll down where it states "Write a Customer Review." Write your review here!

#4: After writing your review, send me an email at Kevin@KevinCSnyder.com and I will reply with an additional special link for FREE stuff!

BONUS!!

Even more ☺

Also, receive your "Daily Dose" of inspiration by downloading my leadership app!

KevinCSnyder

Follow me on your social of choice
@KevinCSnyder

Let's stay in touch!

Made in the USA
Columbia, SC
31 August 2018